The Mind Appliance

HOME COMPUTER APPLICATIONS

T. G. LEWIS

HAYDEN BOOK COMPANY, INC.
Rochelle Park, New Jersey

In Memory of My Father

Would it have been
    that you could see
the tomorrows you lost.

Yes, and were it possible
    to tell you
of their splendor,

I would,
I would

Library of Congress Cataloging in Publication Data

Lewis, Theodore Gyle, 1941
The mind appliance.

Includes index.
1. Electronic data processing. I. Title.
II. Title: Home computer applications.
QA76.L46 001.6'4 78-5411
ISBN 0-8104-5112-3

Printed in the United States of America

3 4 5 6 7 8 9 PRINTING

78 79 80 81 82 83 84 85 86 YEAR

PREFACE

This is an idea book, a book for experimenters, and a book with a simple message: computers can be fun and challenging.

I have selected a collection of applications that represent a cross-section of computing. From the "poetry generating programs" to the "picture drawing" programs, this book is meant to provide an adventure in computing while giving the reader the tools needed for bigger and more sophisticated processing. Many of the concepts were taken from university courses on computing and have been reduced to their essence for ease in understanding and pleasant reading.

The style of the book is motivated by a psychoanalyst's view of computer hobbyists. This tongue-in-cheek approach is meant to entertain and lead the reader into relatively complex programming situations with a mininum of effort. I hope you will read these little episodes with a light-hearted attitude.

The first two chapters discuss basic terms and techniques in a way that should make for easy reading for those in need of an introduction. Although this material is available elsewhere, the subsequent chapters give detailed demonstrations of new material not found in other books. In each section I have tried to give BASIC programs that have actually been run on one of the computers owned and operated by myself. These programs are meant to serve only as a starting point for further software development. Their intent is to show you how to actually implement the techniques advocated.

The later chapters increase in difficulty in many respects. For example, increased mathematical sophistication is necessary for the chapter on graphics, more complicated file access methods are required for the diskette applications, and finally, an 8080 assembler language program for automatic telephone dial-up is given in the last chapter. These difficulties can be mastered in every case with dedicated study and experimentation.

I would be remiss if I did not express my appreciation to the many people who directly and indirectly contributed to this enjoyable project. Dianne Littwin of Hayden Book checked my male chauvinist prose and humor; Henry Ledgard of the University of Massachusetts labored over the material and made many helpful comments. Thanks also go to the Real Oregon Computer Store, Les Moore, Jim Bohle, and Fred Yunker for their assistance with hardware. Also Ms. Homyer once again patiently typed the manuscript with astounding accuracy, Marciel Partridge edited earlier versions, checking my backwoods Oregon grammar before it was released on the world, and Madeline Rubin aided and abetted me when aid was needed.

It is my hope that you enjoy and intellectually prosper from the time spent reading this work.

T. G. LEWIS

CONTENTS

Chapter One

BUYING FOR THE HOME

"And if I'm elected, there will be a computer in every home!" To drive this point home, the speaker pounded the podium with a clenched fist. The crowd roared its approval.

Election year, 1988

There are many reasons to own a home computer: bookkeeping, status symbol, work for profit. Perhaps the best reason is also the most obvious: entertainment. Computing in the comfort of a sofa, den, or near a fireplace is a hobby enjoyed by thousands of Americans. It replaces component stereo hi-fi and experimental electronics equipment as the nation's newest gadget for relaxation and enjoyment. Why?

A computer system offers the ultimate puzzle. Of all the high achievements of technology, it poses the greatest challenge to the human intellect. It appeals neither to our senses nor to physical exertion, but to the most sacred of our possessions: mind.

Stereo sound stimulates our sense of hearing and often appeals to our emotions. Television and motion pictures stimulate our inner fantasies and often appeal to both emotion and intellect alike. Special experiences (football, travel) offer a near brush with contrived worlds. It is the computer, though, that deserves respect beyond any of the escapes mentioned above, because only a computer is able to simulate real and imagined worlds in the way that only pure minds have been able to do in the past. For the first time in history, we have an intellect to be reckoned with that is equal to our own.

A stereo hi-fi may enthrall with the latest innovations in music, but a computer with music generator can push musical invention beyond the boundaries set by the music masters. A television program may keep us on the edge of our sofa for an hour or two, but a computer can keep us on the edge of intellectual suspense throughout the night with a game of Trek or a game of our own invention.

Clearly, humankind has progressed to a new plateau. Behind is a long-reaching upward slope of mechanical achievements, each designed to relieve us of back-breaking or tedious work. These machines are extensions of our body: arms, legs, sight, hearing, and so forth. On this new plateau lies a world of astounding machines—machines that are able to extend our mental capacities. For the first time, we are face to face with the ultimate appliance—the mind appliance.

1.1 Hardware and Software

A computer is a slave. It is designed to do what it is told to do by the programs written by human beings. The manner and form in which these programs are written depend on the two fundamental parts of a modern computer system: *hardware* (the electrical, mechanical, and tangible part) and *software* (the intangible, control part).

I have been asked many times in the past, "What is the best computer system to buy?" My answer has always been, "It depends on what you want to do with it!" I recall an early experience with this question several years ago when Joyce and Rob decided to buy their very first home computer.

Joyce was a systems analyst for a three-letter computer manufacturer. She was knowledgeable about large-scale computers but had no experience with small systems. Rob was a real-estate salesman and pleaded total ignorance of the field. By the time they came to see me, their marriage was threatened by Joyce's involvement with computing. Luckily, I was able to configure a domestic computer that would serve them well for nearly five years.

When I ran into Rob a few months later, he said, "I can't thank you enough for recommending our system. Joyce and I are really close again and enjoying our evenings computing together."

Joyce wanted a computer with a front panel (toggle switches and lights), but Rob felt this was too threatening since he preferred to avoid the details of the machine's operation. Rob's concept was to buy a system with one button (on/off) and interact with the software rather than the hardware.

"But I want to examine main memory and read the contents of registers," Joyce complained. "You always want to fiddle with bits and all that nonsense, Joyce," Rob countered. "I want to use BASIC and get some programs running right away."

Rob and Joyce faced a now classic dilemma. A computer with a front panel lets you check out new additions to a system and interact with the machine at a detailed level. This level of interaction is not essential, as Rob pointed out. The level which you select is actually a matter of taste, as shown in Table 1.1.

Table 1.1 Hardware/software levels in a personal computer

Level	Language	Operating System	Hardware
High	BASIC interpreter FORTRAN compiler	Disk, Tape, Operating System Editor	Keyboard/CRT Power button
Middle	Assembler language	Editor Debugger Loader	Keyboard/CRT Front Panel
Low	Machine language (binary)	Monitor Loader	Front Panel ROM

At the lowest level, every computer has its own language, called the *machine language.* This language is based on binary arithmetic (ones and zeroes). A certain pattern of bits (binary digits) causes the hardware to add, subtract, move or copy data, or perform input.

The system is usually under the control of a monitor that allows you to read a program from type into memory, examine the binary patterns stored inside memory, or simply run a program. The front panel also is useful for starting the computer, entering data or instructions directly into the system, or making certain that the circuitry is working properly.

Often a ROM (read only memory) is used to store essential "start-up" control information in the machine. For example, a ROM bootstrap loader is useful for automatically starting the system when power is turned on.

If Joyce and Rob wanted to interact with their home system at the middle level, they would have to write their programs in a symbolic machine language. For example, instead of inputting a binary number for the addition operation, they would use a *mnemonic* for addition, for example, ADD. This method is easier for them but requires an additional step for the computer.

A program called an *assembler* may be purchased. It is used to translate mnemonics like ADD into machine language. To make it simple to alter the mnemonics in a large program, there is usually another program that can be purchased for this purpose. It is called the *text editor.*

A text editor is used to insert new instructions into an existing program, modify instructions, or delete erroneous instructions. The errors are found with the aid of a debugger program and the front panel.

Finally, a *loader* is useful for copying programs into memory prior to executing them. The loader is also valuable for combining several programs into one program. This procedure, called *linking*, is useful when a program uses other programs that have been separately prepared.

Joyce and Rob argued for several weeks before returning to my office for additional advice.

"He is just too stubborn for me," she cried. "I had a system all picked out and he refused to sign the credit card." Joyce was bawling.

"She is being unfair, just because she thinks she knows so blinking much about computers," retorted Rob in self-defense.

I popped a notorious question. "Well, exactly what do you two want to do with this system?" Before long, we had it all settled.

Joyce and Rob wanted to write application programs for their home. They finally arrived at a compromise. Rob persuaded Joyce to get a "turnkey" system that could be used at a high level. In return, Rob agreed to let Joyce do most of the programming. These are the features that they decided upon, and why:

1. *Language:* They selected BASIC, which is a high-level language with extensions for string processing, files, and functions. Joyce and Rob could not use all these features on their initial system, but eventually they wanted to get a larger system and this choice gave them maximal flexibility. Questions they had to ask were: (a) Does BASIC have strings, string operators, and functions? (b) Does BASIC have random and sequential files? (c) Does BASIC have a PRINT USING statement? (d) Does BASIC fit into a 16K memory? (e) What size programs can be run, and what happens when the programs desired exceed the memory space?
2. *Memory:* They selected a 32K (32,000) byte (character) memory because the software provided for the operating system and BASIC interpreter required 20K, leaving only 12K for programs. Questions they had to ask were: (a) How much memory is required by the "system's software?" (b) Do we need static or dynamic memory, and what is its speed? (c) How much memory will our system hold (maximum capacity)?
3. *Operating system:* They selected a disk operating system because programs and data are stored on a diskette peripheral. Questions they had to ask were: (a) What is the capacity of the DOS (diskette operating system) in terms of number of users (simultaneous), memory requirements, and disk space? (b) What functions can the DOS perform? (c) What file access methods does the DOS possess? (d) Can we extend the DOS, and how?

4. *Storage:* They had a choice between inexpensive cassette tape and more expensive diskette. They chose the diskette peripheral memory because it is faster and provides random and sequential access. These two features are essential for storage of data. The questions they had to ask were: (a) What is the speed and capacity of diskette versus tape? (b) How reliable is each? (c) What is the cost? (d) What software support is available for each (DOS, etc.)?
5. *Terminals:* They could have selected a CRT and a printer, but they decided "hard copy" was not necessary for their home. Joyce and Rob elected to purchase a keyboard/CRT terminal for interaction and communication with their processor. Questions they had to ask were: (a) How much does the terminal cost? (b) What features does each offer, and are the features worth the extra money? (c) What is the reliability of the device?
6. *Processor:* They were stumped by this choice. Since they decided to avoid low-level programming, they selected the processor offering the most software. Questions they had to ask were: (a) What is a processor, and what kinds are available? (b) How much do they cost? (c) Are peripherals available for the processor selected? (d) What is the processor's speed, reliability, and special features?

When they returned for their weekly therapy session, Joyce and Rob were beaming with pride. They had just received their new microcomputer system for their home. They left my office embracing one another, and as far as I know, they are living happily ever after.

This example from my files covered a lot of technical territory in a short time. Let's take a closer look at the terms used in the story above, just to make sure of their meaning. A minimum level of literacy is essential before visiting the local computer store.

We can take an imaginary voyage with Betty Byte, a hypothetical character of information. A *byte* is a unit of information equivalent to a single character from the alphabet or a single numeral from the ten digits. We use the notation "4K bytes," for example, to measure the size of memory capable of holding 4096 bytes. Therefore, 1K = 1024, and we say the computer memory is capable of storing "one-kay bytes" of data.

Betty Byte starts her journey through a personal computer by being typed into the machine through a keyboard. We depress the letter "B" on the keyboard of a terminal and Betty is on her way. Her journey would be the same whether we enter a "B" or a "5," or any other character from the keyboard.

Betty ("B") is copied from the keyboard into the main memory of the personal computer. First, the letter "B" is converted into electrical signals. Actually, the keyboard is connected to an electric circuit that converts the pushed button into eight signals. Each signal is represented by a one or zero (binary number representation), and it is the collection of these eight signals that actually become stored in the personal computer's memory.

A processor (the computer itself) is needed to copy the encoded "B" from the terminal to the main memory. The processor (for example, a Z80, 8080, 6800, or 6502) copies the byte into a location inside the main memory. The processor is instructed to do this by a program that is also stored in the main memory. Therefore, the main memory is the storage unit for running programs and temporary data.

The main memory is made of metal-oxide semiconductor material. The short name for this is MOS. In addition, MOS main memory can be either read-only (ROM) or read-and-write (RAM) memory. ROM stores information that cannot be altered; therefore, it is useful for storing the programs that start up the computer when power is applied. One the other hand, RAM can be changed. It is used to hold programs and data during processor execution of the program. Unfortunately, RAM "forgets" when the power is removed, making it necessary to copy the start-up information from tape or terminal when starting the computer.

Betty Byte is now in MOS main memory . If we want to save her for later use, we must copy her onto a cassette tape, floppy diskette, or some more permanent storage device. The processor can do this only if a program for writing to tape (or diskette) is run. The letter "B", for example, is copied onto tape by sending electrical signals to the tape device. The tape device (or diskette) converts the signals into magnetic spots recorded on the tape.

The journey taken by Betty Byte is typical of the data-processing functions performed by all computers. If Betty Byte is a digit, say "5," then she may have been part of a number, like "258." Numbers must be converted to internal signals that can be added, subtracted, and compared.

If Betty Byte is a letter, say "B," then she may have been part of a *string*, like "BETTY." Strings must be stored in an internal code that distinguishes them from numbers so that they can be connected or *concatenated*, separated, and compared. In the remainder of this book we will demonstrate how to manipulate both numbers and strings.

1.2 Peripherals

Peripherals are the devices that can be connected to a personal computer, allowing it to communicate with people, store large amounts of data, and control other machines. The most exciting combinations of man and machine occur when clever, useful, and novel peripherals are used in conjunction with the versatility of a computer.

A terminal is the simplest peripheral and perhaps the most essential. The keyboard lets you input programs and data. The CRT (cathode-ray tube) screen provides a convenient way for the computer to "talk back." In most cases, communication with a terminal is made in simple English, or with English-like words and phrases.

A diskette or tape device is used to (permanently) store programs and data. In a later chapter we will demonstrate this by developing a program to store cooking recipes for use in a kitchen computer system. The recipes in such a system will be stored on tape or diskette.

The essential difference between a tape and a disk is this: Tape must be searched from one end to the other, whereas a disk can be directly (randomly) accessed without searching. This is an oversimplification, but it demonstrates an important feature of tape and disk that may be valuable in selecting one over the other. If you need frequent and rapid access to data (called "records" when stored on a tape or disk), then the added cost of a disk is worthwhile.

A graphical display peripheral is sometimes used to draw pictures rather than write sentences. In many applications a picture is truly worth a thousand words. In such applications, the added expense of a graphical device is justified.

Two kinds of graphical devices are available: *storage tube* and *refresh tube.* A storage-tube graphical device "paints" a picture on the screen once, and the picture remains until erased. A refresh tube "paints" the picture 30 to 40 times each second, giving the appearance of permanence. A home TV is an example of a refresh graphics device.

A digital camera is used with a graphical device to capture visual data in much the same way as a motion picture camera. The "digital picture" is obtained from a collection of light-sensitive cells inside the camera. The camera converts light signals into electrical signals for processing by computer.

Rob and Joyce were interested in controlling their energy-efficient house with their new personal computer. They connected their computer to the central heating thermostat. They purchased a "sample-and-hold" board to interface the thermostat to their machine.

A *sample-and-hold* interface is an electrical circuit that converts an electrical signal from a continuous form into a digital form. A *continuous signal* is one that changes gradually, such as the electrical current in a wall outlet. A *digital signal* changes abruptly from a "one" to a "zero" or a "zero" to a "one". Computers operate on digital signals, whereas most other electrical devices, for example, heaters, radios, TVs, refrigerators, etc., operate on continuous signals. A continuous signal is said to be an *analog* signal, whereas a digital signal is said to be *discrete.* The sample-and-hold interface converts from analog (A) to digital (D). Therefore, it is called an *A/D converter.*

Rob connected the A/D converter to their system by plugging a sample-and-hold board into the processor box. Then he connected the wires from the heating thermostat to the A/D converter so that the computer could "read" the temperature and "write" the thermostat setting.

Joyce wrote a program to make their personal computer input temperature readings every two minutes and adjust the temperature accordingly. In the morning, the house is gradually warmed, and after breakfast, it is cooled. In the evening when Rob and Joyce return from work, the house is warmed again and ready for their comfort.

1.3 How to Write Programs

The most important considerations in buying a home computer are ease of use and maintenance. Maintenance is provided by a computer store.

The easiest computer to use is one that has already been programmed. A *software package* is a collection of programs, like prerecorded musical tapes. You simply buy a tape or diskette and load it into your home system.

The next best system (for ease of use) is one that can be easily programmed. Unfortunately, writing good programs is a highly skilled art. Good programs are in short supply; therefore, you will most likely end up writing programs for your own applications. We can provide only a quick review of the most fundamental programming techniques. For a complete tutorial on programming in BASIC, consult an appropriate textbook.

There are a few fundamental rules in programming that can help you write programs that work properly. These rules have been developed by professional programmers over years of experience:

1. *Plan:* Use a methodology that best suits your own style, but above all else, *plan.*
2. *Use levels of abstraction:* Set your plan down in black and white. Write and rewrite the plan until you are clear about how to write the program. Do not attempt to write the program until you have refined your plan in steps, each step more precise and detailed than the previous one.
3. *Program in blocks:* Don't attempt to write the entire program in one piece. Instead, design and implement smaller pieces one at a time. Put the pieces together after you are sure each piece works.
4. *Put in checks:* Include checks in your final program to make sure it is running properly.
5. *Simpler is better:* If given a choice between a simple method versus a complicated one, use the simpler method. After the program works, you can change it to make it faster or more versatile.

(A) Highest level program

Input:
Miles
Gallons
Dollars

mpg = miles ÷ gallons
\$ per mile = dollars ÷ miles

Output:
X mpg
\$ Y

(B) Next level program

1. Read input data
2. Store miles in M, gallons in G, and dollars in D.
3. Compute mpg and store the result in X. Also compute dollars per mile and store the result in Y.
4. Output the answers along with the input data as a check.

(C) BASIC program

```
10    INPUT M, G, D
20    LET X = M/G
30    LET Y = D/M
40    PRINT M, G, D, X, Y
50    END
```

Fig. 1.1 Levels of abstraction for gasoline calculation

We will illustrate these rules with a program to compute gasoline mileage. Suppose that we travel 280 miles on 12.6 gallons of gasoline. The gasoline was purchased for \$7.60. What is the mile-per-gallon (mpg) value and the cost per mile?

1. *Plan:* We will use an input/output analysis method. The inputs are 280 miles, \$7.60, and 12.6 gal. The outputs are X mpg, and \$ Y per mile. Our plan is to input the data, compute the X and Y values, and print them out.
2. *Use levels of abstraction:* The highest level of abstraction is shown in the diagram of Fig. 1.1(A). In Fig. 1.1(B), we have refined the highest level abstraction into a program with more detail. In Fig. 1.1(C), the program is ready to run in BASIC.
3. *Program in blocks:* This example is too short to demonstrate this concept, but there are four blocks of concern in programming: statements, loops, choice, and subprograms. Illustrations of each of these fundamental blocks are given in logical form and in BASIC notation (see Fig. 1.2).
4. *Put in checks:* We use the redundant output of M, G, and D as a check in the simple program of Fig. 1.1. We will develop other checks as we continue throughout the book.

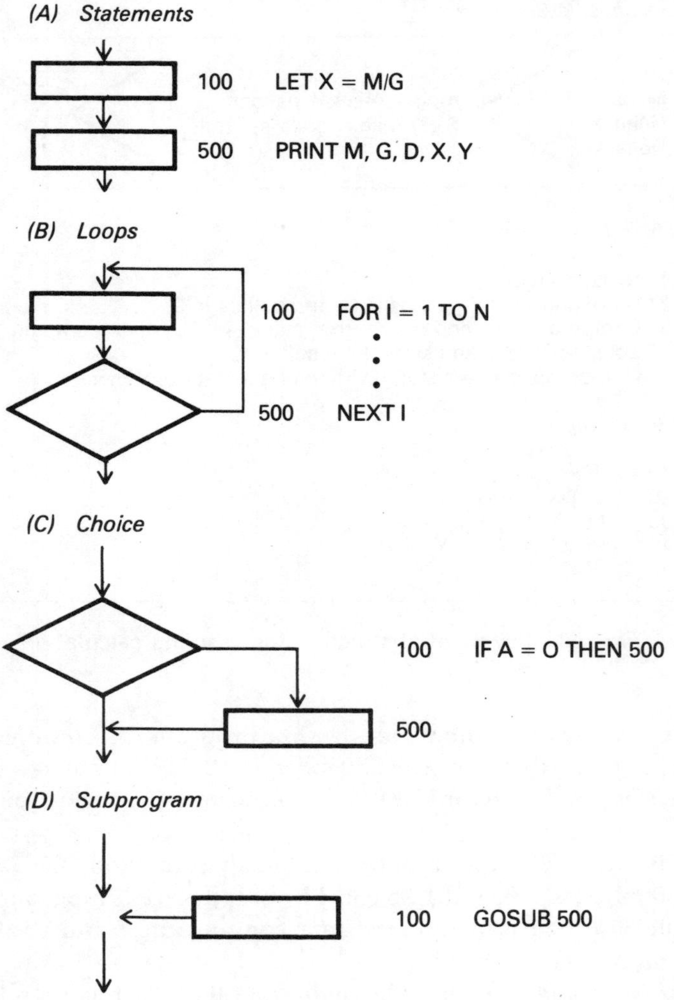

Fig. 1.2 Fundamental building blocks of programming

5. *Simpler is better:* The straightforward, obvious approach to problem solving is the most elegant approach in programming.

In Fig. 1.2 we illustrated the most fundamental building blocks of all programming. In fact, it is only the first three structures that are needed to write any program at all. The subprogram structure in Fig. 1.2(D) is extremely useful, but not essential. We can illustrate these blocks more successfully if we choose an example that uses all four fundamentals.

Suppose that we want to compute the balance remaining from a paycheck after the bills have been paid. We know what amount to start

(A) Highest level

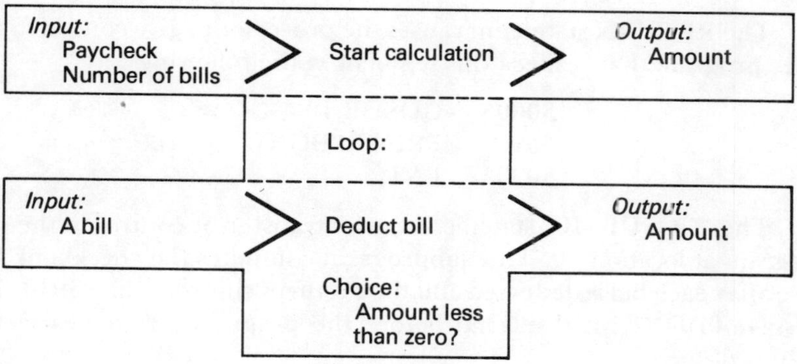

(B) More detail

1. Read P = paycheck, N = number of bills
2. LOOP N times:
    2.1 Read a bill, B
    2.2 Subtract B from P
    2.3 Print B and P
    2.4 If P less than zero, stop
3. Print final balance, P

Fig. 1.3 The bill deduction program

with, and we know that the bills must be subtracted from the beginning amount. We want a program that subtracts each bill from the running balance and that stops after all bills have been deducted, or stops if the balance becomes zero or negative. The levels of abstraction are shown in Fig. 1.3.

The abstractions of Fig. 1.3 can be used to write a simple, straightforward BASIC program that will run on any personal computer. The building blocks consist of BASIC statements,

```
10      INPUT P
20      INPUT N
```

BASIC loops,

```
30      FOR I = 1 TO N
        40      INPUT B
        50      LET P = P - B
        60      PRINT B, P
        70      IF P<= 0 THEN 99
80      NEXT I
```

choice (line 70 above), and finally subprogramming:

```
90      PRINT P
99      RETURN
```

The RETURN statement causes the processor to give control to any other program that "called" this segment in the following way:

```
3000    GOSUB 10
3010    PRINT "DONE"
3020    END
```

The "GOSUB 10" statement causes transfer of control to the subprogram at location 10. This subprogram computes the checkbook balance after each bill is deducted and then returns control to line 3010. The message "DONE" is displayed before the program terminates in line 3020.

The use of statements, loops, choice, and subprograms will be further developed in this book. They are fundamental to all programming, and as such, warrant our detailed attention.

Rob and Joyce wisely chose a version of BASIC that includes many helpful features. A short list of features is given below to help you select the best BASIC for your applications:

1. Floating point arithmetic: for dollars and cents calculations
2. Functions (INT, SIN, SQR, RND, etc.): for calculator mode of operation and convenience
3. Arrays: variables with more than one value per name; DIM statement
4. Strings: variables with $, for handling letters and characters
5. Files: I/O device storage (at least, sequential, random, and possibly indexed access to storage of data)
6. Formatting: PRINT USING and IMAGE statements along with TAB functions to format output
7. Program overlay: APPEND statement for very large programs that must be executed in pieces since they will not fit into main memory.
8. Edit: text editor ability to help in preparing programs
9. Miscellaneous: multiple statements per line to compress programs, indentation for readability, and string functions for manipulation of characters

You are now ready to start using your personal computer. In the next chapter we will present some useful techniques that may help you understand the programs in this book. If you feel comfortable with BASIC, and want to dive into the home applications, then skip Chap. 2.

Chapter Two

THE GARAGE (FUNDAMENTALS OF BASIC)

"The ultimate law of personal computing is that of robotics. The more human a computer system becomes, the more useful it becomes. The difference between humans and machines is where software comes in."

Reflections in a pool, 1978

Mary, a young wife living in an East Coast metropolitan suburb, came to me after two years of suffering. Therapy with several analysts had brought little improvement to her life.

"I just don't know where to turn," she explained in a soft voice. "John is so absorbed with his electronic inventions that I rarely see him anymore."

"Yes, I can understand how you feel," I said in a fatherly tone. She told me her story from beginning to end. A crisp, bright, autumn afternoon gave way to a cool evening under piercing, untwinkling stars.

"As I understand your story"—I paused to light my pipe and think a moment—"your husband has abandoned you in favor of a personal computer. In effect, you have become what is called a 'computer widow.' This is a frequent occurrence in the suburbs. In fact, there are an estimated 10,000 computer widows alive today."

She was sobbing once again. "I feel more like the victim of a computer mistress. John spends more time in the garage caressing his keyboard and S-100 bus than he spends with the family."

Clearly, Mary had to learn computer programming so that she could establish communication with John. I wrote an article for computer widows, gave it to Mary, and, a month later, she returned to see me.

"I'm so much happier now! The two kids and I are helping John develop a program to trace our ancestors and keep track of the family tree. It's very exciting." Mary had recaptured the joy of marriage once again.

Several months later, I found out that Mary had become so enthralled with programming their garage computer that she returned to college to earn a degree in computer science.

2.1 Brush up on BASIC

The BASIC language used in many personal computers was originally developed at Dartmouth College for large time-shared (centralized) computers. The idea behind BASIC was to make programming easy for first-time programmers, for example, students. This is exactly why BASIC is simple and popular.

There are many dialects of BASIC. Each dialect has features not found in all versions of the language. Therefore, it is difficult to explain every possible feature without causing confusion. The discussion of BASIC given here is actually only a beginner's description intended to get you started. Additional commands, and more details, can be obtained by reading the manual supplied with each personal computer system.

Every BASIC statement has two important items at the beginning: (1) a number, and (2) a *keyword.* The numbered statements must be in ascending order so that the personal computer can recognize the proper location of each statement within the program. The keyword is a word used to tell the personal computer what function to perform. Here are a few of the most important statements, and what they do:

10	REM	Remark, for annotation of a program
15	INPUT	Input a number, name, etc.
18	PRINT	Output a number, name, etc.
20	LET	Copy the value of an expression to a specified storage location
21	IF and THEN	Test a comparison and jump to another statement, regardless
50	GOSUB	Run a subprogram, then return to the next statement following 50
60	RETURN	Return from a subprogram
70	STOP	Stop a program
90	FOR and NEXT	Repeat a group of statements

In addition, most personal computers equipped with BASIC provide a set of commands for manipulating entire BASIC programs. A list of typical commands is given below:

RUN	Execute, or "run," a program stored in the main memory
GET or LOAD	Copy a program from tape or disk into the main memory (get it ready to RUN)
PUT or SAVE	Copy a newly entered program from main memory to tape or disk (save it so that it can be used again)
LIST	Print-out a copy of the program (used to see what the program in memory looks like)
EDIT	Change the program (allows you to modify one or more statements)
REN	Renumber the statements of a program
SCR	Scratch, or erase a program from main memory

An example will help you understand these commands. Suppose that we want to compute the price-per-unit of a grocery item. For example, is soap cheaper at $1.09 for the Giant Economy Package of 12 oz, or at $2.15 in the Amazing Sale Price version containing 25 oz?

The following dialogue with a personal computer occurred on June 23, 1977. (The underlined items are responses obtained from the computer.)

```
:
:   10   REM COMPUTE PRICE PER UNIT
:   20   REM
:   30   INPUT "ENTER PRICE", D
:   40   LET X = D/U
:   RUN
?
```

At this stage in the dialogue, the program is (incorrectly) entered into the main memory and an attempt is made to run it. The question mark signifies that the system is waiting for the user to type an input value into the computer through the running program. This value is stored in D when entered. Suppose that we input D equal to 1.09:

```
1.09
UNDEFINED VARIABLE AT LINE 40
```

The computer stops executing the program because of the error at line 40. We would probably execute a list (LIST) to see what the program looks like before attempting to fix it. Next, we would insert the corrections by defining an input value for variable U:

```
:   35   INPUT "UNITS", U
:   45   PRINT "PRICE/UNIT =", X
:   60   STOP
:   RUN
```

This time the program will complete the execution and terminate with the message,

STOP IN LINE 60

Enter this program into your home computer and see which soap bargain is best.

The program above is simple and easy to write with very little experience. The other programs in this book require a much more sophisticated approach to programming. The hints given in Chap. 1 are most highly recommended. They are so important, in fact, that we shall repeat the check list here:

1. Plan
2. Use levels of abstraction
3. Program in blocks
4. Put in checks
5. Simpler is better

The reader is encouraged to study the example in Chap. 1 in greater detail before continuing. A BASIC programming book may also be useful.

Continuing with the program just discussed, suppose that we want to save it for use at a later date. Most systems allow you to name your program so that it may be remembered and retrieved. For example, the command,

```
:   SAVE PRICE
```

or one similar to it will cause the program to be named and copied to disk or tape.

The command,

```
:   GET PRICE
```

will retrieve the program so that it may be run once again. The command,

```
:   NEW
```

will clear memory of all statements and allow you to enter a new program from scratch.

Often, the programs you want run are too long to fit into main memory. When this happens, you may use the overlay capability provided by many versions of BASIC. A CHAIN or APPEND command is useful for bringing pieces of a program into memory one at a time. The command,

```
:    APPEND PRICE
```

will cause program PRICE to be attached to the end of the (current) program already in main memory.

2.2 Input/Output Tools

The most difficult parts of BASIC are the statements that do input and output. It is in this area that the dialects of BASIC vary greatly. We classify I/O statements into two categories: (1) terminal I/O, and (2) mass storage I/O.

Terminal I/O

Terminal I/O is used to communicate between a user and the computer system's terminal device(s). The keyboard, CRT, and printer comprise a typical system.

In programming for mass storage I/O, we instruct the computer to communicate with a storage device like tape or disk. A disk or tape is organized into files. Each file has one or more records, and each record contains any number of numbers or characters. In BASIC, we must read or write a record of information from, or to, the device.

We have already seen a simple example of terminal I/O when we traced the path of a byte through a keyboard. A segment of BASIC code for displaying ten lines of "Not Tonight, Josephine" is shown below:

```
10    REM DEMO CRT DISPLAY
20    FOR I = 1 TO 10
30    PRINT "NOT TONIGHT, JOSEPHINE"
40    NEXT I
```

Suppose that we want a permanent copy of this message printed on paper instead. How can we direct this message to the printer? Here is a situation where dialects of BASIC differ. In most versions you can replace line 30 with a statement similar to the one below:

```
30    PRINT @ 33: "NOT TONIGHT, JOSEPHINE"
```

The "@ 33:" phrase signals BASIC to direct the output to device 33. In this case, device 33 happens to be a printer.

Formatting is one of the problems faced by terminal I/O. When the following segment of BASIC is executed, most personal computers will output 0.100000 E 1, or a similar general form for 1.0:

```
105    LET X = 1.0
115    PRINT X
```

This situation is particularly annoying when the number represents dollars and cents. A typical dollars and cents calculation requires only two digits to the right of the decimal sign. Formatting is accomplished in BASIC with the PRINT USING statement or its equivalent:

```
105    LET X = 1.0
115    PRINT USING 120:X
120    IMAGE 3D.2D
```

Again, the form of the IMAGE statement may differ from one version of BASIC to another. In the example above, the output is 1.00, because 3D.2D means to place two digits to the right and three digits to the left of the decimal point. Note that statement 115 uses statement 120 as a format statement.

Finally, we can direct the formatted output to a printer:

```
115    PRINT @ 33: USING 120:X
120    IMAGE 10X, 3D.2D
```

The 10X format causes ten spaces to appear before the value of X is printed.

Mass Storage I/O

Tape I/O and disk I/O are as radically different in BASIC as terminal I/O and mass storage I/O. The reason is simple: The devices work differently and hence must be handled differently.

Tape I/O is sequential, that is, we can never change a record in the middle of a file without reading from the beginning to the end of the file. The following code produces records that look like the records in Fig. 2.1:

```
1100   FOR I = 1 TO 10
1105   PRINT @ 31:A, B, C
1110   NEXT I
```

Simply stated, the tape file places each record next to the previously written record. To retrieve Record 2, for example, we must program the computer to search for the second record by first reading the beginning record.

A further restriction on tape is this: To rewrite (change) a record on tape, we must rewrite the entire file. The gaps between records on tape [see Fig. 2.1(A)] serve as "start" and "stop" cushions. Rewriting a record would require an exact match between the old record and the new record. Since the tape device is rarely accurate enough to rewrite between two

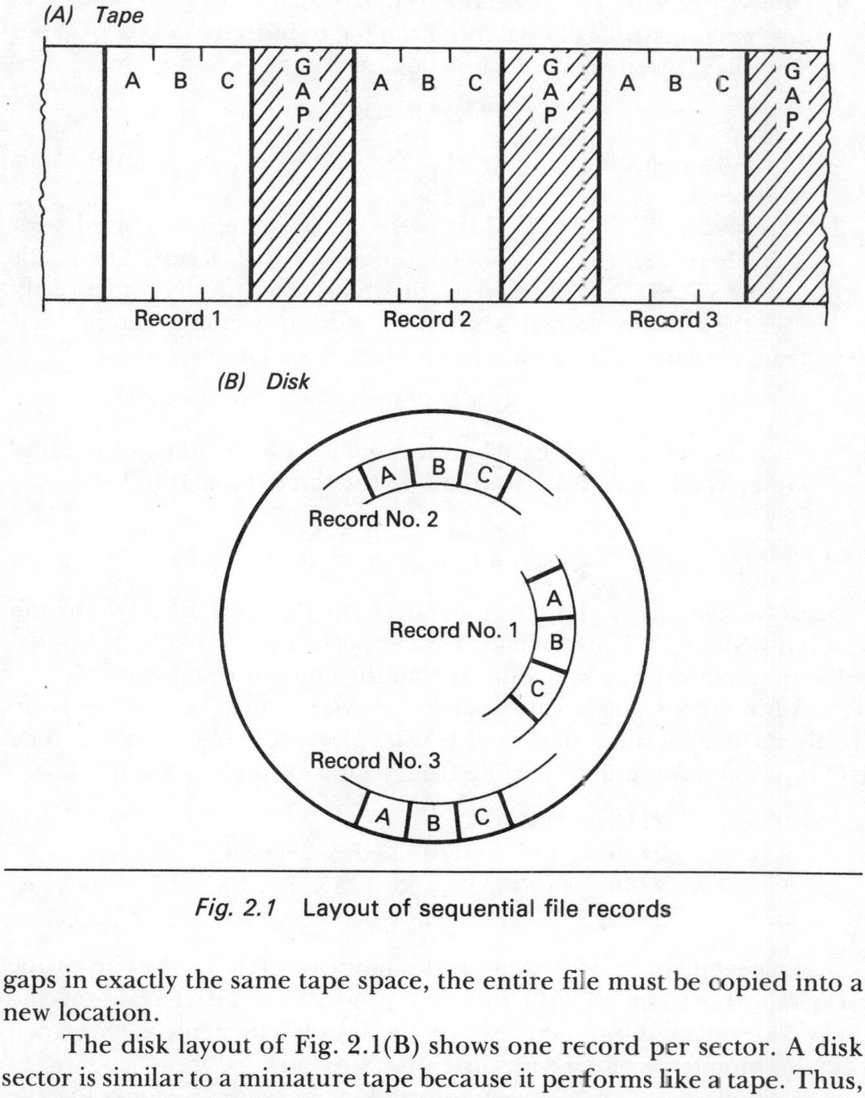

Fig. 2.1 Layout of sequential file records

gaps in exactly the same tape space, the entire file must be copied into a new location.

The disk layout of Fig. 2.1(B) shows one record per sector. A disk sector is similar to a miniature tape because it performs like a tape. Thus, when the record containing A, B, and C is written to a disk sector, the random access nature of the rotating disk allows an update in any order we choose.

Unfortunately, the disk sector may be too small or too large for the record. In such a case, we either waste memory or we must split records—part on one sector, part on another sector.

Manipulation of mass storage files is complicated further by three other functions that must be performed before an actual read/write is possible:

1. *OPEN or FIND:* This operation is performed before any other I/O operation in order to establish if the file is, indeed, on disk or tape. The file is often equated with a logical name:

   OPEN #1, "DATA"

   This example shows how the file, "DATA," is assigned unit Number 1.
2. *RESTORE, %, or FIND (disk, only):* This operation is used with disk when performing a random (nonsequential) access. The result of a RESTORE is to position the disk read/write mechanism directly over the sector or record to be read or written. Sectors are numbered from zero to some maximum number. For example,

   RESTORE #1, 58

   prepares sector number 58 in file Number 1 for reading or writing. Other versions of BASIC would do the same thing as follows:

   FIND #1, 58, A, B, C
   READ #1, %58, A, B, C

3. *CLOSE or END:* This command closes an open file. Often, the CLOSE or END statement writes a special end-of-file (EOF) signal on the tape or disk to indicate that the end has been reached.

Additional details about a particular system must be gleaned from the user's manual since dialects of BASIC play a big role in mass storage I/O capability. A segment of code from a tape example is given below:

```
2110    FIND 2
2120    ON EOF(0) THEN 2350
2130    INPUT @ 33: I, A$, B$, C$
2140    GOTO 2120
```

This segment of BASIC illustrates how to search for the end-of-file on a tape file. The EOF(0) function produces a TRUE value if the end-of-file mark is reached. Notice the input statement; each record contains an integer along with three character strings.

A similar search mechanism for random access to disk looks like the following.

```
2105    LET I1 = 0
2110    OPEN #2, "DFILE"
2120    ON EOF(2) THEN 2350
2130    RESTORE #2, I1
2135    READ #2, I, A$, B$, C$
2140    LET I1 = I1 + 1
2145    GOTO 2120
```

This example shows how to simulate a sequential file on a disk. The variable I1 actually "points to" the sector containing record number I1.

Be sure to read the manual of your own personal computer to see how each of these functions is performed.

2.3 Storage Tools

BASIC has three types of storage elements. Any of the three elements are used to input, output, or process data. In fact, each type of storage element can be stored on disk, tape, or in main memory. As programmers, we must be careful to separate each type of data and use special functions in BASIC when the data type requires it.

Simple Variables and Numbers

The most common type of data in BASIC is called *numeric data.* A number is an example of numeric data:

1
1.5
0.1E3
–1.399999

We use the LET statement to process numeric data. For example, suppose we compute the average of N numbers using LET, IF, and FOR statements, as shown in Fig. 2.2. The program of Fig. 2.2 illustrates several concepts covered in this chapter. First, the terminal I/O functions are used to prompt the user and print on device D1 (which is defined before running the program). The PRINT USING and IMAGE statements illustrate control of output format.

Strings and Names

Quite often it is convenient to store and process alphabetical data rather than numeric data. This need is provided for in BASIC through the use of string variables. A string variable is any variable that:

1. Appears in a DIM statement
2. Terminates with a $

As an example of a string variable, suppose we store both the first and last names of a person in a string array, N$. We use several functions built into BASIC to manipulate the name string, as follows:

LEN Returns the length (number of characters) of a string as the value of LEN

```
100 REM*********************************************
110 REM
120 REM  compute avg.,max., and min. of n numbers
130 REM
140 REM*********************************************
150 REM
160 PRINT "enter the number of numbers:";
170 INPUT N
180 REM
190 REM-----assume min and max----------------------
200 REM
210 LET M0=-99999.99
220 LET M1=99999.99
230 REM
240 REM-----find real min and max-------------------
250 REM
260 LET S=0
270 FOR I=1 TO N
280 PRINT "enter a number";
290 INPUT X
300 IF X>M0 THEN 360
310 IF X<M1 THEN 410
320 GO TO 450
330 REM
340 REM-----just found a bigger one-----------------
350 REM
360 LET M0=X
370 GO TO 450
380 REM
390 REM--------just found a smaller one----------------
400 REM
410 LET M1=X
420 REM
430 REM--------in either case, sum x----------------------
440 REM
450 LET S=S+X
460 NEXT I
470 REM
480 REM----------calculate average, a-----------------
490 REM
500 LET A=S/N
510 REM
520 REM----------output them-------------------------
530 REM
540 PRINT @D1: USING 550:" ave=",A," min=",M1," max=",M0
550 IMAGE 5a,5d.2d,5a,5d.2d,5a,5d.2d
560 STOP
```

Fig. 2.2 Numeric processing

&, +	Concatenates (adds) one string to another
REP	Replaces one substring with another substring. The replaced substring is lost.
POS	Finds the (integer valued) position of a substring in a string

```
100 REM**************************************************
110 REM
120 REM         reverse first and last names
130 REM
140 REM**************************************************
150 REM
160 DIM N$(20),F$(19),L$(19),T$(1)
170 LET F$=""
180 PRINT "enter first name, then last name:";
190 INPUT N$
200 REM
210 REM---------find space--------------------------
220 REM
230 FOR I=1 TO 19
240 LET T$=SEG(N$,I,1)
250 IF T$=" " THEN 290
260 LET F$=F$&T$
270 NEXT I
280 REM
290 REM--------copy last name to first--------------
300 REM
310 LET L$=SEG(N$,I+1,LEN(N$))
320 LET N$=L$&","
330 LET N$=N$&F$
340 REM
350 REM--------print it-----------------------------
360 REM
370 PRINT "last name, first name is:",N$
380 STOP
```

Fig. 2.3 String processing example

SEG Extracts a substring from a string

Examples of these functions in action are briefly given below. Study these examples before reading the program in Fig. 2.3.

```
100   DIM A$(10), B$(5), C$(5)
110   LET B$ = "BBBBB"
120   LET C$ = "CCCCC"
130   LET A$ = B$ & C$
```

The result in A$ at statement 130 is "BBBBBCCCCC". The values stored in C$ and B$ are unaltered. The result of the statement,

```
200   LET J = POS(A$, "CCC", 1)
```

is that J is 6 because the three "C's" begin in character position 6 of string A$. The result of the statement,

```
300   LET A$ = REP("XYZ", 3, 3)
```

is to replace the three characters starting in position 3 of A$ = "BBBBBCCCCC" with "XYZ". The answer is A$ = "BBXYZCCCCC".

The statement,

```
400    LET B$ = SEG(A$, 2, 3)
```

causes B$ to contain "BXY" since the parameters in SEG specify the extraction of a substring from A$. The beginning of the substring is character 2, and the length of the substring is 3 characters.

Finally, study the next example to see how the first and last characters of string A$ are extracted, concatenated, and stored in string C$:

```
500    LET C$ = SEG(A$, 1, 1) & SEG(A$, 10, 1)
```

The sample program in Fig. 2.3 locates the separating space between the first and last name stored in string N$. The names are reversed (last name first, first name last), and a comma is placed between them.

The routine in Fig. 2.3 could be used to store a list of frequently called telephone numbers, given each person's last name. Such a program is left as an exercise for the reader.

2.4 Game Tools

Many of the programs written for home entertainment are game programs. Simulated space flight, gambling, guessing, and graphical games all depend upon a pseudo random number generator, RND. This function is called *pseudo random* because it is not truly random. In fact, RND is computed from a formula similar to the one below:

$$\text{NEW RND} = A * \text{OLD RND} + C \qquad \text{Modulo } M$$

$$A = 1 \qquad \text{Modulo } 4$$
$$C = 1 \qquad \text{Modulo } 2$$
$$M = 2^S \qquad S > O$$

The modulo calculation means to divide and take the remainder left after division. For example, suppose M = 8, A = 5, and C = 1. Then, given a *seed* OLD RND of 3, say, the sequence generated by repeated application of the formula produces "pseudo" random integers between 0 and (M–1).

$$\begin{aligned}
&\text{OLD RND} = 3 \\
&\text{NEW RND} = (5)(3) + 1 && \text{Modulo } 8 = 0 \\
&\text{NEW RND} = (5)(0) + 1 && \text{Modulo } 8 = 1 \\
&\text{NEW RND} = (5)(1) + 1 && \text{Modulo } 8 = 6 \\
&\text{NEW RND} = (5)(6) + 1 && \text{Modulo } 8 = 7 \\
&\text{NEW RND} = (5)(7) + 1 && \text{Modulo } 8 = 4 \\
&\text{NEW RND} = (5)(4) + 1 && \text{Modulo } 8 = 5 \\
&\quad\vdots
\end{aligned}$$

The first calculation above is given in detail below to illustrate the modulo calculation:

```
100 REM************************************************
110 REM
120 REM         a pseudorandom number generator
130 REM
140 REM************************************************
150 REM
160 REM      new=a*old+c  modulo m
170 REM
180 LET A=33
190 LET C=1
200 LET M=512
210 LET X=3
220 REM
230 REM
240 FOR I=1 TO M
250 LET X=A*X+C
260 LET X=INT(X-M*INT(X/M))
270 LET R=X/M
280 PRINT R
290 NEXT I
300 REM
310 REM------------------------------------------------
320 REM
330 STOP
```

Fig. 2.4 BASIC version of RND

$$
\begin{aligned}
(5)(3) + 1 &= 15 + 1 \\
&= 16 \quad \text{Modulo } 8 \\
&= (16/8) \quad \text{Modulo } 8 \\
&= 2 + \text{remainder } 0 \quad \text{Modulo } 8 \\
&= 0 \quad \text{Modulo } 8
\end{aligned}
$$

Notice that a starting value is specified in advance (OLD RND). After this is done, we can produce all numbers in the sequence without added inputs.

A BASIC program for calculating pseudo random numbers in the range of zero to one is given in Fig. 2.4. We have used the INT function to chop off the decimal fraction. The calculations yield the remainder after division by M; they do so by means of the statement,

LET X = INT(X–M * INT(X/M))

For example, when X is 31 and M is 8, the calculation produces:

$$
\begin{aligned}
&= 31-8*(3) \\
&= \ 7
\end{aligned}
$$

Since every number is known to be less than M, we produce numbers between zero and one by a final division:

LET R = X/M

```
100 REM**********************************************
110 REM
120 REM        SHUFFLE 52 ITEMS
130 REM
140 REM**********************************************
150 REM
160 DIM D(52)
170 REM
180 FOR I=1 TO 52
190 LET D(I)=I
200 NEXT I
210 REM
220 REM-------------SELECT RANDOM CARD-----------
230 REM
240 FOR I=52 TO 1 STEP -1
250 LET K=INT(RND(1)*I)+1
260 LET T=D(I)
270 LET D(I)=D(K)
280 LET D(K)=T
290 NEXT I
300 REM
310 REM-------------PRINT 'EM--------------------
320 REM
330 FOR I=1 TO 50 STEP 3
340 PRINT @41:D(I),D(I+1),D(I+2)
350 NEXT I
360 REM
```

Fig. 2.5 Card shuffle program

Figure 2.4 will generate 511 pseudo random numbers before any numbers are repeated.

The RND function is built-in in most versions of BASIC. Therefore, to use RND, we merely need to "call" it by name, as shown in the card shuffle program of Fig. 2.5. Here is how the program works.

A deck of cards is stored in an encoded array of numbers (see the DIM statement). The cards are numbered from 1 to 52. An array is a BASIC variable that:

1. Appears in a DIM statement along with its length [for example, DIM A(50)]
2. Is accessed by name and subscript value [for example, LET X = A(J)]

We want to shuffle the array holding numbers from 1 to 52. The algorithm is as follows:

1. Store the numbers 1 to 52 in locations 1 to 52 of the "deck" array.
2. Start with the last element of the array, element N, in general. (a) Select a random subscript from 1 to N, and (b) exchange the last element (the Nth one) with the randomly selected element.
3. Shorten the deck by one, and repeat with (N−1) "cards" in the deck.
4. When N=1, stop.

The algorithm above shuffles the deck in as few steps as possible. It uses 51 pseudo random numbers computed by RND. The argument of RND causes the next number in the sequence to be selected each time RND is computed.

2.5 Number Tricks

The final section in this review of BASIC describes several useful functions found in most versions of BASIC. These functions can save many hours of programming if used properly.

ABS Returns the number with a positive sign attached. It is most often used to test two numbers to see if they are approximately equal. The example below shows how we can test for two numbers that may be within E of one another.

```
450     IF ABS((X-Y)/X)<E THEN 550
```

SGN Returns (+1) if its argument is greater than zero and (−1) otherwise. We could use it to see if a number is even or odd, for example:

```
380     IF SGN(X-2*INT(X/2))>0 THEN 500
```

RND Returns a pseudo random number between zero and 1

SQR Returns the square root of its argument

INT Returns the largest integer possible without a decimal fraction.

Additional functions are found in many versions of BASIC, but they are not "standard." Some of the "nonstandard" functions used in this book are listed below:

PAGE	This clears the screen of all output
DRAW	This draws a straight line from the current point on a screen to the specified point on the screen
MOVE	This moves a graphics cursor from its current position to the specified point on the screen. It does exactly what DRAW does, except that no line is drawn.
WINDOW	This sets up a user's scale for graphics.
VIEWPORT	This selects a section of the screen for viewing from the entire screen.
TYP	This tests the tape or disk controller to see what its status is.
EOF	This tests the tape or disk for an end-of-file mark.

We put the INT function to use in order to illustrate how helpful a

```
100 INIT
110 REM*****************************************************
120 REM
130 REM          give change
140 REM
150 REM*****************************************************
160 DIM T(10),D(10)
170 LET D(1)=20
180 LET D(2)=10
190 LET D(3)=5
200 LET D(4)=1
210 LET D(5)=0.5
220 LET D(6)=0.25
230 LET D(7)=0.1
240 LET D(8)=0.05
250 LET D(9)=0.01
260 REM
270 REM
280 PRINT "enter dollars and cents of purchase";
290 INPUT D1
300 PRINT "amount paid in dollars and cents";
310 INPUT A
320 REM
330 REM------compute change----------------------
340 REM
350 LET B=A-D1
360 IF B=>0 THEN 450
370 REM
380 REM------not enough !-----------------------
390 REM
400 PRINT "please give me more money!!!!"
410 GO TO 270
420 REM
430 REM------compute size of bills---------------
440 REM
450 PRINT USING 460:"your change is:",B
460 IMAGE 15a,3d.2d
470 REM
480 REM------count it out-----------------------
490 REM
500 FOR I=1 TO 9
510 LET T(I)=INT(B/D(I))
520 LET B=B-T(I)*D(I)
530 IF B<=0.009 THEN 640
540 NEXT I
550 REM
560 REM----------------------------------------
570 REM
580 IF B<=0.009 THEN 640
590 PRINT "out of change--come back later."
600 STOP
610 REM
620 REM------print results-----------------------
630 REM
640 FOR J=1 TO I
650 IF T(J)=0 THEN 680
660 PRINT USING 670:T(J)," in ",D(J),"'s"
670 IMAGE 3d   ,4a,3d.2d,2a
680 NEXT J
690 STOP
```

Fig. 2.6 Point-of-sale program

function can be in an application. Suppose that we now write a program that computes change for an electronic cash register. The answer tells a clerk how many dollar bills, quarters, nickels, and dimes to give a customer after a purchase.

This program will be found in Fig. 2.6, which illustrates the usefulness of arrays as well as of INT. The D array is used to store each denomination of coins. We successively divide the total by D(I) and take the quotient as the number of coins to return.

Figure 2.6 gives a program that should be part of every intelligent cash register today. Intelligent cash registers are called point-of-sale (POS) terminals.

Chapter Three

THE LIVING ROOM (SIMPLE RETRIEVAL)

"I had a dream . . . I was dressed in black leather pants, knee-high boots, and a very chic silver blouse . . . kinda like in a science fiction movie about the future. When I walked into my living room, soft lights grew brighter in cool intensity, melting the shadows. And there in the middle of the room was a huge white egg. I must have done this a thousand times before. As I approached the egg, it opened in the middle like a flip-top cigarette package. Inside was a luxurious chair surrounded by controls, a TV screen, and a microphone. I stepped into my egg-shaped personal computer. It closed, and I spent the next several hours in a simulated world, more fantastic than a dream."

Alice reminisces

Alice was a self-made woman when she celebrated her thirtieth birthday. Men followed her around at work, gazed at her form during luncheons, and performed feats beyond reporting just to escort her to social events. It was not only because of her beauty, although that was a part of it. Nor was it entirely due to her abilities. What Alice had I am not sure anyone can accurately describe beyond the single word, "charisma."

The corporation where Alice worked valued her contribution beyond the contributions of all other executives. In fact, she was the first vice-president to reach that echelon before turning 30. She would most likely have reached her goal of being a vice-president and director of research before turning 30 even if she had failed to finish college before her eighteenth birthday, which, of course, she did not.

We illustrate the basic linear search strategy below. This BASIC program segment assumes that the list is stored in array L and that the key is stored in variable K:

```
10     DIM L(100)
..     ...
80     INPUT K
100    FOR I = 1 TO 100
110    IF L(I) = K THEN 300
120    NEXT I
130    REM ----- NO MATCH FOUND ----
140    PRINT "NO MATCH FOUND"
150    LET I = 0
160    RETURN
300    REM ---- FOUND AT I ----
310    PRINT "FOUND AT", I
320    RETURN
```

The linear search continues to compare every item in the list, L, until either the item equal to K has been found or the list has been exhausted.

A tape file is searched in the same way as a BASIC array. The segment of code below parallels the earlier example, but notice the difference:

```
10     FIND 1
15     REM ----- OPEN TAPE FILE #1 -----
       ...
80     INPUT K
100    FOR I = 1 TO 100
105    INPUT @ 33: L
110    IF L = K THEN 300
120    NEXT I
130    REM ----- NO MATCH -----
140    PRINT "NO MATCH FOUND" -----
150    LET I = 0
160    RETURN
300    REM ----- FOUND AT I -----
310    PRINT "FOUND AT", I
320    RETURN
```

Throughout this chapter and the next, we will study other methods for searching files. These methods are useful in disk systems because disks provide for *direct* rather than sequential access (correspondingly, they are not useful for tape systems). In direct access, any item in a list (file) can be directly accessed without reading the file from beginning to end.

Suppose, for example, that we have the following ordered list stored in a disk file. Each number is stored in a physical record called a *sector*. The disk access mechanism that is needed to directly access sector number K, say, depends upon physical sectoring. Most physical sectors contain either 128 or 256 characters of storage space. In addition, the sectors are numbered from zero to an upper limit analogous with an array in BASIC:

Sector 0 : 18 ←———————— START
Sector 1 : 25
Sector 2 : 32
Sector 3 : 33
Sector 4 : 35
Sector 5 : 36
Sector 6 : 42
Sector 7 : 49 ←———————— STOP

The list above is ordered, from small to large values. We can use a very fast search procedure when the list is ordered and direct access is permitted. The *binary search* scheme works as follows.

The first item compared with key K is the middle item of the list. Suppose the list is located between sectors START and STOP. The middle item is INT((START + STOP)/2). In the example above, the middle item searched first is in sector INT((0 + 7)/2), or sector 3.

Suppose that we want to locate K = 35 in the illustration. We begin with sector 3. Since 33 is not equal to 35, the match fails. We know, however, that every item before sector 3 is less than 33. Therefore, we discard the first one-half of the list from further consideration (35 must be in the last half of the list).

We let START equal 4 and repeat the search by computing a new middle element:

Sector 4 : 35 ←———————— START
Sector 5 : 36 ←———————— MIDDLE
Sector 6 : 42
Sector 7 : 49 ←———————— STOP

Again, the MIDDLE item does not equal K; instead, 36 is larger than K. We can use this information to discard every item beyond sector 5 from further consideration. This leaves only one item in the list. Thus, we need only one more comparison to find K = 35:

Sector 4 : 35 ←—START ←—STOP ←—MIDDLE

The binary search required only three comparisons to search eight items. This is a vast improvement over the linear search, but of course we paid a price: The list must be ordered and stored on a direct-access device.

Returning to the application at hand, we want to store each TV program according to two numbers. The Julian date, beginning with the date of the first TV log entered, and the time-of-day are used to store and retrieve the programs of channels 2, 5, and 9.

Suppose, for example, that we enter the TV program schedule for 08/10/77, as shown in Fig. 3.2. Imagine that this log is entered on 08/03/77, one week earlier than the scheduled programs. Thus, 08/03/77 is the beginning date of data entry, and the tape contains logs for 08/03/77, 08/04/77, . . . 08/10/77, etc.

We compute the Julian date equivalent of 08/03/77 and subtract it from the Julian date equivalent of the look-up log date, 08/10/77. This produces a difference of 7 days.

Next, we compute the hour of the day from noting in Fig. 3.2 that the log begins at 18:00 o'clock. Hence, the first program is at "logical time" zero, the second program at "logical time" one, and so forth. The formula below computes the "logical time" given the 24-hour clock time:

```
100    INPUT "HOURS:", H, "MINUTES:", M
110    LET TI = INT (H-18) + INT (M/30)
```

The resulting "index" into the TV log of Fig. 3.2 is computed by adding the two variables together:

```
200    LET I1 = L*R + T1
```

where:

L = Julian date
R = number records in each log
I1 = logical time

The value of L above is obtained in a manner equivalent to that used for L in Fig. 3.1. In the hypothetical example posed here, the value of L is 7. Hence, to index into the logical time of 08/10/77 at 20:30, we must compute as follows:

H = 20
M = 30
T1= INT ((20-18)) + INT (30/30)
   = 5
L = 7 (from Julian date calculation)
T1= 7*9 + 5
   = 68

The value of R(R = 9) used in this example refers to the number of entries in each daily log. The daily logs of each day (08/03/77, 08/04/77, 08/05/77 . . . 08/10/77, 08/11/77, . . .) is assumed to follow the pattern in Fig. 3.2. Therefore, we assume nine half-hour slots for each log.

The half-hour slots in Fig. 3.2 contain information that must be stored on tape or disk. We learned earlier that searching tape differs considerably from searching disk. Now we can see where the difference comes in.

If we implement the TV log system on a tape storage personal computer, the search for index item I1 equal to 68 appears similar to the linear search program:

```
100     FIND 5
110     FOR I = 1 TO (I1-1)
120     INPUT @ 33: H, M, A$, B$, C$
130     NEXT I
```

This segment of code reads (68–1) records. Each record contains the information from a horizontal line in the TV log stored on tape drive 33. The FIND 5 command opens file 5 on the tape, and skips files 1, 2, 3, and 4. Once the file is opened, 67 records are read, one at a time, into H(hours), M(minutes), A$(channel 2 show), B$(channel 5 show), and C$(channel 9 show). Each of these records is thrown away because it is not the record being searched for.

When we use tape, it must be read in order to be positioned at the beginning of the look-up record:

```
140     INPUT @ 33: H, M, A$, B$, C$
150     PRINT
160     PRINT H, M, A$, B$, C$
```

Record 68 is finally accessed and printed for the user. Often we must close the file before actual printing occurs because of the possible buffering of the records as they are taken from the tape:

```
170     CLOSE 5
```

A *buffer* is a region of main memory used to temporarily store records while they are waiting to be written onto a storage device (output) or read into program variables (input). Buffers help to speed up data processing when there is a speed difference between memory and tape or disk.

If we elected to store the TV log on a diskette instead of tape, we would have a choice between sequential and direct access methods of retrieval.

The disk-sequential access method appears to be identical in BASIC to the tape-sequential access method. Economy of space is one reason for using sequential access even when employing disk storage.

In order to perform direct access, each record (H, M, A$, B$, C$ in our example) is indexed with a record number. The record number is used in a manner similar to that for the subscript of an array.

To convert the look-up procedure of the TV log example for use with direct-access diskette storage, we must assign a record number to each record. Suppose that we have a diskette with 350 sectors numbered from 0 to 349. We can allocate the sectors as follows: Record I1 is placed in sector (I1 – 1).

Most dialects of BASIC provide a direct-access mechanism to specify the sector (record) number before a read or write. One method uses the modified RESTORE command approach:

```
 90    OPEN #35, 1
100    INPUT "HOURS:", H, "MINUTES:", M
 ..    ....
410    RESTORE #(I1-1)
420    INPUT #35: H, M, A$, B$, C$
430    CLOSE #35, 1
440    PRINT H, M, A$, B$, C$
```

This segment of code accomplishes a direct access to record (I1 – 1) stored on device 35. Another version of this follows:

```
 90    OPEN #35, 1
100    INPUT "HOURS:", H, "MINUTES:", M
 ..    ....
410    REM GET RECORD I1
420    READ #35; (I1-1): H, M, A$, B$, C$
430    CLOSE #35, 1
440    PRINT H, M, A$, B$, C$
```

Note that, in the version above, READ is used instead of INPUT to signify an external device other than a terminal keyboard.

The syntax of BASIC may vary from the dialects illustrated here, but the concepts are the same in all versions allowing direct access. *Random access* and *direct access* are also identical in operation. They are different names for the same access method.

The programs for automated TV log storage and retrieval are straightforward in their implementation once the access methods of tape or diskette are understood. A program called BUILD is needed to build the log file. Another program called RETRIEVE is needed to do the retrieval.

3.3 Sports Statistics Retrieval

The TV log program of the previous section is part of the TV entertainment module that Alice designed for her egg and illustrates a few simple techniques for storing information on tape and disk.

Next, we want to illustrate how to index alphabetical data in a manner similar to that used for the numerical data already shown. To make this section interesting, we will use a sports statistics retrieval system as an example.

Our sports statistics program is designed to give access to information concerning athletes. The feature that makes this kind of retrieval different from that used for the TV log is the use of alphabetical as well as numerical keys. For example, given the name "Walton," we might learn (retrieve) that he is a basketball player with so many points to his credit, a certain defensive record, and perhaps his height.

Suppose that we develop a program to store names and batting averages of famous baseball players. The input (BUILD) program accepts a name and an average. The name is used to locate the proper record, and once located, the average is stored with the name.

The retrieval program (LOOK-UP) accepts a name and retrieves the correct batting average. Both name and average are printed. How can we use alphabetical information such as a name to directly access a record in a file?

We will show how to perform the direct look-up using arrays instead of files on a diskette. This approach is less confusing, but remember that the method applies to any direct-access storage device. The programs given work equally well for access to diskette records. Only the BASIC access code needs to be changed to make these programs work for diskettes.

The first step in designing a name access method is to hash the names into numbers. A *hashing function* is an algorithm that converts a string, or number, into a subscript, or record number. Typically, the record number is much smaller than the possible values taken on by the original number.

The most common hashing function for converting a "large" number into a "smaller" number is the *prime division hash.* It works by computing the remainder left after division by a prime number. The prime number must be equal to the length of the file (in records). We can compute both quotient and remainder of a number as follows:

```
150     LET Q = INT(N1/N)
160     LET R = INT(N1-Q*N)
```

The order in which the two assignment statements above are executed is most important. The quotient, Q, is easily computed by stripping off the decimal fraction resulting from division of N1.

Suppose that N1 = 25 and N = 11; then the quotient calculation produces Q = 2. The value of N*Q is 22, and when the calculation for R is performed in the next step, the difference between 25 and 22 provides the remainder, 3.

It is important to realize that R ranges from zero to (N−1). Therefore,

$$1 \leq R + 1 \leq N$$

and every remainder produced by division falls in the range of "smaller" numbers. The subscript value R is exactly what is needed to directly access the Rth record of a file containing N records.

Unfortunately, the value of R produced in this manner often fails to be unique, and thus there may be more than one "larger" number N1 that produces identical values of R. For example, with N = 11, we can get R = 0 from N1 = 11, N1 = 22, N1 = 33, and so forth. When this occurs, we compute an offset number to use as a second attempt to locate a unique record (or subscript).

The most common offset number in practical use is the quotient, Q. Thus, the second probe into the file will be at sector R + Q. The third probe will be at R + 2Q, and so forth.

The records in each case are checked to see if they are the matching records when compared with the search key. If R is used to locate a record and the search key does not match the record's key, the offset calculation, R + Q, is used to continue the search.

We can reduce a large number to a smaller number with prime division. The problem of reducing a large string, or name, to a small number is still with us. How can we convert a baseball player's name into a number, R?

The ASC and SEQ functions are useful for this purpose. The ASC function converts a letter of the alphabet into an integer between 65 and 92. The SEG function extracts a letter from a string when used as follows:

```
310    LET X$ = SEG(N$, J, 1)
```

The SEG function above removes the Jth letter from N$ and stores it in X$. We employ this function over and over again, from J = 1 to the LENGTH of N$, in order to extract every letter, one at a time, from N$.

When the prime division hash and the name conversion algorithms are combined, we get the subprogram shown in Fig. 3.3. Note how the value returned in place of each letter of N$ is weighted by J and summed to obtain I1. This method *almost always* produces a unique value I1 in place of a name.

The hashing function uses three arrays for each record. The values in F refer to the availability of an entry in the file space. If F = (−1), the record (sector) is free for use, and if F = (+1), the record is occupied. The value of I1 for each name is stored in array S. This is a necessary condition to guarantee a match between I1 and S during a look-up. The data—in this case a batting average—is stored in a third array (not shown in Fig. 3.3) called A.

The hashing routine is used to build a file (insert) when F1 = 1 and to retrieve a record when F1 = (−1). Thus, using F1 allows us to employ the hashing function routine for both insertion into the file and retrieval from the file.

The file build and file look-up routines are greatly simplified when

```
1000 REM*******************************************
1010 REM
1020 REM         HASHING FUNCTION
1030 REM
1040 REM*******************************************
1050 REM
1060 REM   N$ IS THE NAME KEY , GIVEN
1070 REM   I1 IS THE KEY EXPRESSED AS AN INTEGER
1080 REM   N  IS THE TABLE LENGTH AND DIVISOR
1090 REM   F  IS THE ARRAY OF FLAGS FOR THE INDEX
1100 REM      WHERE (-1) MEANS EMPTY,
1110 REM      AND   (+1) MEANS FULL
1120 REM   F1 IS AN ACTION CODE, (-1) MEANS LOOK-UP,
1130 REM      AND (+1) MEANS INITIAL INSERTION
1140 REM   R  IS THE RETURNED SUBSCRIPT RETRIEVED
1150 REM   S  IS THE DATA ARRAY, CONTAINING I1
1160 REM
1170 REM ------COMPUTE I1-------------------------
1180 REM
1190 LET I1=0
1200 FOR J=1 TO LEN(N$)
1210 LET X$=SEG(N$,J,1)
1220 LET X=ASC(X$)-65
1230 LET I1=I1+J*X
1240 NEXT J
1250 REM
1260 REM ----------PERFORM HASH------------------
1270 REM
1280 LET Q1=INT(I1/N)
1290 LET R1=INT(I1-Q1*N)
1300 LET R=R1+1
1310 LET Q=Q1+1
1320 REM-----------REPEAT COMPARISONS-------------
1330 FOR J1=1 TO N-1
1340 IF F(R)>0 THEN 1380
1350 IF F1>0 THEN 1480
1360 LET R=0
1370 RETURN
1380 REM-----------COMPARE WITH KEY---------------
1390 IF S(R)=I1 THEN 1480
1400 LET R=R+Q1
1410 LET Q=INT(R/N)
1420 LET R1=INT(R-Q*N)
1430 LET R=R1+1
1440 NEXT J1
1450 REM-----------ERROR EXIT--------------------
1460 LET R=0
1470 REM-----------NORMAL EXIT-------------------
1480 RETURN
```

Fig. 3.3 Subprogram

hashing is used. We can pass a name (through N$) to the routine, and, when F1 = 1, we are in a position to add a new name and batting average to the file. We can set F1 = (–1) and pass a name to the routine to get data back.

```
100 REM*********************************************************
110 REM
120 REM BUILD BASEBALL BATTING AVERAGE STATISTICS FILE
130 REM
140 REM*********************************************************
150 REM
160 LET N=11
170 DIM N$(10),F(N),S(N),A(N),X$(1)
180 FOR J1=1 TO N
190 LET F(J1)=-1
200 NEXT J1
210 LET F1=1
220 REM
230 REM-----------GET NAME--------------------------------------
240 REM
250 PRINT "ENTER PLAYERS NAME:";
260 INPUT N$
270 IF N$<>"" THEN 300
280 PRINT "END OF FILE BUILD PROGRAM"
290 STOP
300 REM
310 REM------------HASH NAME TO INDEX, R--------------------
320 REM
330 GOSUB 1000
340 IF R>0 THEN 370
350 PRINT "ERROR---FILE FULL"
360 STOP
370 REM
380 REM------------INPUT BATTING AVG.-----------------------
390 REM
400 PRINT "ENTER BATTING AVERAGE:";
410 INPUT A(R)
420 LET F(R)=1
430 LET S(R)=I1
440 REM
450 REM------------GET ANOTHER ONE--------------------------
460 REM
470 GO TO 230
480 REM
```

Fig. 3.4 File build program

The file build program is shown in Fig. 3.4, and the look-up program is shown in Figure 3.5. In each case, the programs illustrate simple access to the file (arrays in our simplified versions) by first calling the hashing function and then changing F, S, and A.

The programs of Figs. 3.3 through 3.5 can be adapted to disk reads and writes in place of array access by modifying the segments of code dealing with array access. In the next chapter, we will present several BASIC programs that directly manipulate files.

We have studied only a few of the many access mechanisms available for storing and retrieving records. These and other methods were employed in the Egg constructed by Alice. The last report on the Egg project

```
500 REM*****************************************************
510 REM
520 REM    LOOK-UP BASEBALL PLAYER BY NAME
530 REM
540 REM*****************************************************
550 REM
560 PRINT "ENTER PLAYERS NAME:";
570 INPUT N$
580 IF N$<>"" THEN 610
590 PRINT "END OF LOOK-UP PROGRAM"
600 STOP
610 REM
620 REM-----------HASH FOR R--------------------------------
630 REM
640 LET F1=-1
650 GOSUB 1000
660 IF R>0 THEN 700
670 PRINT "THAT NAME NOT FOUND, TRY ANOTHER"
680 GO TO 560
690 REM
700 REM----------OUTPUT STATISTICS-------------------------
710 REM
720 PRINT USING 730:N$,A(R)
730 IMAGE "PLAYER ",10A," HAS BATTING AVG. OF ",1D.3D
740 REM
750 REM----------DO IT AGAIN------------------------------
760 REM
770 GO TO 560
780 REM
```

Fig. 3.5 Look-up program

was a rumor that Alice was on the verge of connecting the Egg to a telecommunications system. The system is going to teleport her to work each day, making it unnecessary for her to leave the Egg.

Chapter Four

THE KITCHEN (ADVANCED RETRIEVAL SYSTEMS)

"Roger, what do you want for dinner tonight? Shall I press the casserole button or the beef stew button?"

Roger and Mable in Computerland

Roger was dutiful, loyal, and obedient, that is to say, a good husband. He provided a quiet, respectable home in the suburbs for Mable and their two children, Swartz and Lolabear. But when Mable insisted on replacing her kitchen with the newest personal computer kitchen, Roger rebelled.

"Mable, you are crazy," he shouted over his shoulder. Roger was so upset that he didn't realize that he was pacing back and forth in front of their big bay window in his underwear. "You must be practical."

"Oh, Roger, you don't understand. A personal computer in the refrigerator will help me plan meals and go shopping. An intelligent stove will save us money on food. A computerized cupboard will save me time in finding recipes. I could go on and on, dear!" She was upset, too. Roger had promised to remodel their old house, and he should think ahead. After all, remodeling only happens once in a long while.

"Mable, I'm warning you, if you bring those damn computers into *my* home, I'll, I'll . . . I don't know what I'll do." Roger felt he should assert himself as the head of the household.

A few months later, I talked to Roger and Mable. They had remodeled their kitchen and their intelligent appliances were doing fine.

"I don't know how we got along, before," Roger bubbled.

We sat in their living room while the rain danced overhead. Roger and Mable told the story so often that they bored everyone with the details of how they wrote their recipe retrieval system.

4.1 The Recipe System

Roger and Mable's retrieval system stores recipes on magnetic tape. Recipes are retrieved by means of a numeric key that represents the foods used in the meal. Since the two of them are concerned about good nutrition, the foods are divided into four categories according to their nutritional value. Figure 4.1 illustrates these four categories.

Fiber	Fruits and Vegetables	Protein
1. Bread (flour)	1. Citrus	1. Beef or Pork
2. Oats	2. Melon	2. Poultry
3. Rice	3. Juices	3. Fish
4. Corn	4. Greens	4. Eggs
5. Macaroni	5. Reds & Yellows	5. Beans
6. Noodles	6. None of these	6. Nuts
7. Spaghetti		7. None of these
8. None of these		

Dairy Products
1. Milk
2. Cheese
3. None of these

Fig. 4.1 Nutritional categories for the recipe system

The idea behind the retrieval system is rather simple, but the method used to organize the retrieval is more advanced. Each meal is prepared from a recipe stored on tape. Beef Stroganoff, for example, is made from noodles (#6), beef (#1), sour cream (#3), and no fruits or vegetables (#6). We identify the recipe for beef Stroganoff by specifying these four numbers: 6, 1, 3, 6.

FOOD (6, 1, 3, 6) = beef Stroganoff

Similarly, Spanish rice contains foods 3, 1, 3, 4, chili con carne is made of 8, 1, 3, 5, and egg foo yung of 8, 4, 3, 4. In short, the foods that are used to prepare a dish determine the keys to the recipes stored in an "intelligent cupboard" tape system. Thus, we retrieve the beef Stroganoff recipe by inputting 6, 1, 3, 6 in the program (using a prompting display).

The program for storing and retrieving recipes is too large to fit into the small memory of Roger and Mable's intelligent cupboard. Therefore,

```
100 REM**********************************************************
110 REM
120 REM                MAIN PROGRAM FOR RECIPE SYSTEM
130 REM
140 REM**********************************************************
150 REM
160 DIM A$(72),B$(72),C$(72),D$(72),E$(72)
170 REM
180 FIND 6
190 APPEND 1000,10
200 REM
210 PRINT "SELECT ONE OF THE FOLLOWING:"
220 PRINT
230 PRINT "1.INPUT RECIPES          2.OUTPUT ALL RECIPES"
240 PRINT "3.FIND A RECIPE          4.STOP"
250 PRINT
260 PRINT "ENTER CHOICE (1 TO 4)?";
270 INPUT F
280 IF F=>4 THEN 520
290 REM
300 REM----------OVERLAY THE PROPER ROUTINE-----------
310 REM
320 GOSUB F OF 370,420,470
330 GO TO 200
340 REM
350 REM---------------------------------------------
360 REM
370 REM-----------OVERLAY INPUT RECIPES ----------------------
380 FIND 3
390 APPEND 2000,10
400 GOSUB 2000
410 GO TO 200
420 REM-----------OUTPUT RECIPES----------------------
430 FIND 4
440 APPEND 2000,10
450 GOSUB 2000
460 GO TO 200
470 REM-----------LOOKUP A RECIPE --------------------
480 FIND 5
490 APPEND 2000,10
500 GOSUB 2000
510 GO TO 200
520 STOP
540 REM          OVERLAY  AREA
1000 REM         FEATURE INPUT ROUTINE
2000 REM         OVERLAY AREA
```

Fig. 4.2 Appending

it is broken into segments called *overlays.* Each overlay is *appended* to the main program when needed.

Appending in BASIC is accomplished in a variety of ways. Sometimes called *chaining*, it may require special BASIC commands. Often, the RUN command is used to append, but in the program shown in Fig. 4.2, the "APPEND # location, # step" command is used:

\# location = the beginning statement number used to place the first statement
\# step = the incremental step value for subsequent statement numbers

The main program of Fig. 4.2 does the following things: Strings A$, B$, C$, D$, and E$ are used to store five lines of recipe. These five lines are written on tape after inputting a recipe; or, if a recipe look-up is requested, the recipe is read from tape into the five strings.

In lines 180–190 we see an example of opening a tape file (#6), reading a subprogram, and loading it into locations 1000, 1010, 1020, ... This subroutine is used to input foods selected for a menu.

The four items displayed in lines 200–290 illustrate how a user selects one of four program functions. Number 1 allows all input to be done. The input is keyed according to the food features of a recipe and saved in a tape record. Number 2 is used to look up recipes, given its food features, and number 3 is used to output all recipes.

After selecting the function to be performed, the BASIC program of Fig. 4.2 branches to one of three APPEND commands. The proper subprogram is appended at location 2000 of the program, and execution continues. Notice how locations 2000, 2010, . . . , are used by three separate subprograms saved in files #3, #4, or #5. This is the idea behind overlays: Three different segments of program use the same locations of memory but at separate times.

Suppose we select #1 from the menu displayed by the main program. The APPEND command of line 390 overlays the routine shown in Fig. 4.3. Let's study this routine to see how it handles reading tape and how a process called *interrupt* is used.

Lines 2110–2150 must be studied carefully. In line 2110, we open tape file #2, which contains the stored recipes. In this dialect of BASIC, we *enable* an interrupt in line 2120 with the ON condition. Line 2120 specifies that normal program execution be interrupted if an end-of-file (EOF) mark is found during a tape read operation. At any time, if an end-of-file mark is found, then control passes to the *interrupt routine* at 2350. The interrupt routine at 2350–2440 simply turns off the EOF flag and returns control to the line *immediately after* the line causing the interrupt. In this case, since line 2130 may trip an exception (interrupts cause exceptions), the interrupt routine returns to line 2140 after turning off the EOF flag.

Statements 2130–2140 repeatedly execute until the end-of-file mark is discovered by an interrupt or the TYP(0) function. If TYP(0) = 1, then line 2170 is executed next; otherwise control returns to 2130. This code causes the machine to read the existing recipe file until the end is reached. We can insert additional records at the end of the file, thus leaving earlier records unaltered.

```
2000 REM
2010 REM*****************************************************
2020 REM
2030 REM          input recipes onto file 2
2040 REM
2050 REM*****************************************************
2060 REM
2070 REM--------------BUILD MASS STORE FILE-------------
2080 PRINT "ENTER RETURN WHEN READY TO CONTINUE:";
2090 INPUT A$
2100 REM------------FIND END OF FILE--------------------
2110 FIND 2
2120 ON EOF (0) THEN 2350
2130 INPUT @33:I,A$,B$,C$,D$,E$
2140 GO TO TYP(0) OF 2170,2130,2130,2130
2145 GO TO 2170
2150 REM
2160 REM------------INPUT RECIPE AND FEATURES----------
2170 REM
2190 PRINT "DO YOU WANT TO ADD RECIPES ?(YES/NO):";
2200 INPUT A$
2210 IF A$="NO" THEN 2340
2215 PRINT "IDENTIFY RECIPE WITH FEATURES, FIRST"
2216 PRINT "ENTER RETURN WHEN READY TO GO:";
2217 INPUT A$
2220 GOSUB 1000
2230 PRINT "ENTER 5 LINES ONLY, OF RECIPE"
2240 INPUT A$
2250 INPUT B$
2260 INPUT C$
2270 INPUT D$
2280 INPUT E$
2290 PRINT @33:I,A$,B$,C$,D$,E$
2300 REM
2310 PAGE
2320 GO TO 2170
2330 REM----------------AGAIN ??-----------------------
2340 CLOSE @33:
2345 RETURN
2350 REM*************************************************
2360 REM
2370 REM            INTERRUPT ROUTINE
2380 REM
2390 REM*************************************************
2400 REM
2410 OFF EOF (0)
2420 REM-----------SERVE EOF TRAP---------------------
2430 RETURN
2440 REM
```

Fig. 4.3 Input overlay from File #3

The EOF interrupt is needed in this program to take care of a unique situation. The first time the routine is used, the tape file is empty. There are no records to be read; thus, the INPUT command fails immediately. While tripping the EOF flag, the interrupt also sets TYP(0) to 1; hence, we escape from the "error" condition and proceed to write the first recipe.

```
2000 REM
2010 REM**************************************************
2020 REM
2030 REM           OUTPUT RECIPES FROM FILE 2
2040 REM
2050 REM**************************************************
2060 REM
2070 PRINT "STRIKE RETURN WHEN READY TO GO:";
2080 INPUT A$
2090 REM
2100 REM-------------READ 2 FROM BEGINNING-------------
2110 REM
2120 FIND 2
2130 ON EOF (0) THEN 2360
2140 INPUT @33:I,A$,B$,C$,D$,E$
2150 GO TO TYP(0) OF 2350,2180,2180,2180
2160 GO TO 2350
2170 REM
2180 PRINT @Q:"RECIPE #",I
2190 PRINT @Q:
2200 PRINT @Q:"- - - - - - - - - - - - - - - - - - - - -"
2210 PRINT @Q:
2220 PRINT @Q:A$
2230 PRINT @Q:B$
2240 PRINT @Q:C$
2250 PRINT @Q:D$
2260 PRINT @Q:E$
2270 PRINT @Q:
2280 PRINT @Q:
2290 PRINT @Q:
2300 PRINT @Q:
2310 PRINT @Q:
2320 GO TO 2140
2330 REM
2340 REM------------REACHED EOF------------------------
2350 RETURN
2360 REM**************************************************
2370 REM
2380 REM           INTERRUPT ROUTINE FOR EOF
2390 REM
2400 REM**************************************************
2410 REM
2420 OFF EOF (0)
2430 RETURN
2440 REM---------------------------------------------------
```

Fig. 4.4 Output overlays for recipes

Lines 2170–2320 continue to read recipes from the terminal and write them out to the tape file (device #33, line 2290). Finally, when no more inputs are desired, the program CLOSEs the file at device #33, and RETURNs to main.

Figure 4.4 illustrates a similar program for outputting all recipes from file #2. The tape file is opened (line 2120), read from the beginning to the end-of-file mark, and displayed on device Q. If Q is a CRT, we get

```
RECIPE #        648
- - - - - - - - - - - - - - - - - - - - - - - - - - - - - -
        BEEF STROGANOFF—SAUTE 1/2C. ONIONS, 1 CLOVE GARLIC, IN 1/
OVER MED. HEAT. ADD 1 LB GR. BEEF AND BROWN. ADD 2 TBSP. FLOUR, SALT,
PEPPER, AND 1 LB. MUSHROOMS, COOK 5 MIN. STIR IN 10-OZ CAN CREAM O'
CHICKEN SOUP. SIMMER 10 MIN. STIR IN 1C. SOUR CREAM. HEAT THRU, AND
SPRINKLE WITH PARSLEY. SERVE WITH NOODLES (4 TO 6 SERV.).
```

Fig. 4.5 Output of a recipe from tape

each recipe displayed on a terminal screen. If Q is a printer, we get a permanent record similar to that in Fig. 4.5.

The look-up routine of Fig. 4.6 also operates like the other tape I/O routines. The tape is searched sequentially from beginning to end. In line 2210, we compare I to J to see if the keys match. If the value I matches the key stored on tape, J, the record is displayed on device Q.

The input routine resides at location 1000 (see Fig. 4.7). This routine is used in two places in this system. First, it is used each time a new recipe is entered onto tape. The GOSUB 1000 statement in line 2220 (Fig. 4.3) is used to index the new recipe. For example, the index for beef Stroganoff (6, 1, 3, 6) is 648. (How is this computed?)

The input routine is also used to compute index 648 when retrieving the recipe for beef Stroganoff from tape. We can see how the retrieval system works by a careful study of Fig. 4.7.

Lines 1070–1435 merely prompt input from a user. The categories of food of Fig. 4.1 are displayed, and the input consists of a number for each category. Again for beef Stroganoff, the inputs are 6, 1, 3, 6. In Fig. 4.7, these inputs are stored in variables F, P, D, and V:

$$F = 6$$
$$P = 1$$
$$D = 3$$
$$V = 6$$

These four values are put into a formula that converts them into a single number. The formula is a *hashing function* similar to the functions illustrated in the previous chapter. (See Chap. 3 if you are confused.)

The formula works as follows: The maximum values of F, P, D, and V appear in the menus.

$$FMAX = 8, PMAX = 7, DMAX = 3, VMAX = 6$$

We want to produce a unique index, say any number computed from (6, 1, 3, 6), that cannot be computed from (1, 6, 3, 6) or (6, 1, 6, 3), or any other combination of these numbers. We can do this by assigning a weight to each digit in the set, 6, 1, 3, 6.

```
2000 REM
2010 REM*****************************************************
2020 REM
2030 REM           LOOKUP RECIPES FROM FILE 2
2040 REM
2050 REM*****************************************************
2060 REM
2070 PRINT "STRIKE RETURN WHEN READY TO GO:";
2080 INPUT A$
2090 GOSUB 1000
2100 REM
2110 REM--------------READ 2 FROM BEGINNING---------------
2120 REM
2130 FIND 2
2140 ON EOF (0) THEN 2420
2150 INPUT @33:J,A$,B$,C$,D$,E$
2160 GO TO TYP(0) OF 2410,2190,2190,2190
2170 GO TO 2410
2180 REM
2190 REM------------DO THEY MATCH?--------------------
2200 REM
2210 IF I=J THEN 2240
2220 GO TO 2150
2230 REM
2240 PRINT @Q:"RECIPE #",J
2250 PRINT @Q:
2260 PRINT @Q:"-  -  -  -  -  -  -  -  -  -  -  -  -  -  -  -  -  -  -  -  -"
2270 PRINT @Q:
2280 PRINT @Q:A$
2290 PRINT @Q:B$
2300 PRINT @Q:C$
2310 PRINT @Q:D$
2320 PRINT @Q:E$
2330 PRINT @Q:
2340 PRINT @Q:
2350 PRINT @Q:
2360 PRINT @Q:
2370 PRINT @Q:
2380 GO TO 2150
2390 REM
2400 REM-------------REACHED EOF--------------------------
2410 RETURN
2420 REM*******************************************************
2430 REM
2440 REM           INTERRUPT ROUTINE FOR EOF
2450 REM
2460 REM*******************************************************
2470 REM
2480 OFF EOF (0)
2490 PRINT "END OF RECIPE FILE"
2500 RETURN
2510 REM-------------------------------------------------
```

Fig. 4.6 Look-up routine for a recipe

$$
\begin{aligned}
I = {} & WEIGHT_f * (F-1) \\
& + WEIGHT_p * (P-1) \\
& + WEIGHT_d * (D-1) \\
& + WEIGHT_v * (V-1)
\end{aligned}
$$

```
1000 REM*******************************************
1010 REM
1020 REM        INPUT FEATURES OF RECIPE
1030 REM
1040 REM*******************************************
1050 REM
1060 PAGE
1070 PRINT "ENTER NUMBER OF CHOICE :"
1080 PRINT "         FIBRE FOODS"
1090 PRINT
1100 PRINT "1.BREAD (FLOUR)      2.OATS"
1110 PRINT "3.RICE               4.CORN"
1120 PRINT "5.MACARONI           6.NOODLES"
1130 PRINT "7.SPAGHETTI          8.NONE OF THESE"
1140 PRINT
1150 PRINT "ENTER CHOICE (1 TO 8)?";
1170 INPUT F
1180 PAGE
1190 PRINT "         PROTEIN"
1200 PRINT
1210 PRINT "1.BEEF               2.POULTRY"
1220 PRINT "3.FISH               4.EGGS"
1230 PRINT "5.BEANS              6.NUTS"
1240 PRINT "7.NONE OF THESE"
1250 PRINT
1260 PRINT "ENTER CHOICE (1 TO 7)?";
1270 INPUT P
1280 PAGE
1290 PRINT "          DAIRY"
1300 PRINT
1310 PRINT "1.MILK     2.CHEESE     3.NONE OF THESE"
1320 PRINT
1330 PRINT "ENTER CHOICE (1 TO 3)?";
1340 INPUT D
1350 PRINT
1360 PRINT "          FRUITS & VEGETABLES"
1370 PRINT
1380 PRINT "1.CITRUS              2.MELON"
1390 PRINT "3.JUICES              4.GREENS"
1400 PRINT "5.YELLOWS & REDS      6.NONE OF THESE"
1410 PRINT
1420 PRINT "ENTER CHOICE (1 TO 6)?";
1430 INPUT V
1435 REM
1440 REM---------------COMPUTE ID NUMBER--------------
1450 REM
1460 LET I=126*F+18*P+6*D+V-150
1480 RETURN
1500 REM
```

Fig. 4.7 The feature extraction input routine

Each digit is reduced by one because we want their values to lie between zero and one less than their maximums. This assures a unique result for I.

Let us set each weight according to the product of the maximum values, up to, but not including, the maximum of F, as follows:

$$\begin{aligned} WEIGHT_f &= PMAX * DMAX * VMAX = 126 \\ WEIGHT_p &= DMAX * VMAX = 18 \\ WEIGHT_d &= VMAX = 6 \\ WEIGHT_v &= 1 = 1 \end{aligned}$$

We substitute these values in the formula and then reduce it by factoring out the constants:

$$\begin{aligned} I &= 126*(F-1) + 18*(P-1) + 6*(D-1) + V \\ &= 126*F + 18*P + 6*D + V - 150 \end{aligned}$$

We can now compute the index value for beef Stroganoff (6, 1, 3, 6):

$$\begin{aligned} I_B &= 126*(6) + 18*(1) + 6*(3) + 6 - 150 \\ &= 648 \end{aligned}$$

Thus, beef Stroganoff is assigned a simple unique number which incorporates all the information relating to the ingredients needed for its preparation.

The method we have just illustrated is useful in more sophisticated disk systems. Here is the reason why: The index, 648, for example, may be used to pinpoint the record containing the recipe for beef Stroganoff directly. When 648 is used along with a disk file, we do not need to search every record as we did with the tape system. Hence, the disk retrieval of recipes with many features becomes rapid and efficient.

We can turn now to a more advanced form of disk retrieval to illustrate the power of data structures and advanced disk techniques.

4.2 A Disk Chore Chart

Roger and Mable use their intelligent cupboard to keep track of chores as well as recipes. The chore chart programs operate on a disk file, however, rather than a tape file. In fact, storing records on disk allows them to take advantage of direct access in order to speed the search.

First, we must study the basic disk read and write operations used by Roger and Mable. These are illustrated in Fig. 4.8. File READ and File WRITE may be done in either the *sequential mode* or *random* (direct) mode. The examples of Figure 4.8(a) and (b) are done in sequential mode.

The data are taken from string A$ and placed into a sequential file called DATA. The OPEN statement initializes *logical* file #1 to begin accepting output (input) on the *physical* file, DATA.

The TYP(1) function is printed to illustrate how it returns values that can help simplify programming file I/O. If TYP(1) = 0, the next record is an EOF mark. Otherwise TYP(1) = 1.

In the file write routine, EOF = 0 because each WRITE to file stores a record on disk. It also causes an EOF mark to be written following the newly written record.

(A) The sequential Write-DISK Routine

```
100   REM *****************
110   REM
120   REM     FILE WRITE ROUTINE
130   REM
140   REM *****************
150   REM
160   DIM A$ (80)
170   OPEN #1, "DATA"
180   FOR I = 1 TO 10
190       INPUT "ENTER YOUR NAME:", A$
192       IF A$ = "  " THEN END
194       WRITE #1, A$
200       PRINT TYP(1)
210   NEXT I
220   REM - - - - - - - - - - - - - - -
230   CLOSE #1
240   PRINT "DONE"
250   END
```

(B) The sequential Read-DISK Routine

```
100   REM *****************
110   REM
120   REM     FILE READ ROUTINE
130   REM
140   REM *****************
150   REM
160   DIM A$ (80)
170   OPEN #1, "DATA"
180   FOR I = 1 TO 10
190       READ #1, A$
200       PRINT A$
205       PRINT TYP(1)
210   NEXT I
220   REM - - - - - - - - - - - - - - -
230   CLOSE #1
240   PRINT "DONE"
250   END
```

Fig. 4.8 Sequential write-DISK and read-DISK routines

In the file read routine, every READ produces a TYP value of 1 after every READ except the last READ. When TYP = 0, the last record has been read, and the read loop should cease.

In this particular disk BASIC, we can also execute direct access to records regardless of their position in the file by inserting a %K modifier into the READ/WRITE commands:

```
READ  #1 %K, A, B
WRITE #1 %K, A, B
```

These BASIC commands cause the machine to access the Kth record directly (starting from zero) and either read or write the values of A and B.

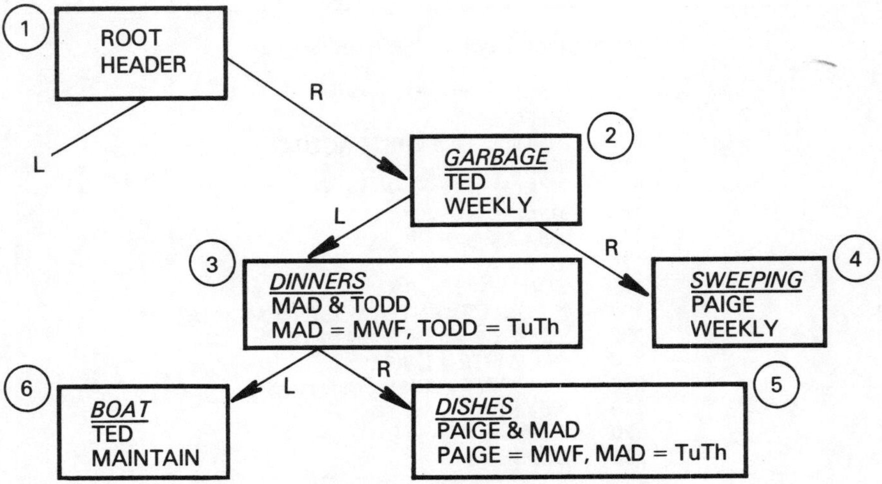

Fig. 4.9 Database trees for chores (record numbers in circles; keys underlined)

Suppose that each variable requires five characters of disk space; then the record containing A, B is 10 characters long. We must advance the value of K by 10 to skip over the characters in each record. Thus, the following code performs like a sequential read routine except that it uses direct access.

```
10    FOR I = 0 TO 100
20    READ #1 %10*I, A, B
30    NEXT I
```

Now let us return to Mable's chore chart problem. Recall that the objective is to access a particular record rapidly without having to search the entire list of records.

The chore chart program uses a chore name as the key to each chore. Each chore record contains the slave's name and a brief comment about the task. Figure 4.9 illustrates a tree-like chore chart containing GARBAGE, DINNERS, SWEEPING, BOAT, and DISHES as chores for PAIGE, TODD, MAD, and TED. We call the tree of Fig. 4.9 a *database tree*.

A database tree is ordered according to the alphabetical order of its keys. Thus, when we look at the root HEADER of Fig. 4.9, we see that everything to the left of GARBAGE comes before GARBAGE (alphabetically). Everything to the right of GARBAGE (that is, SWEEPING) comes after GARBAGE in alphabetical order.

The alphabetization of a database tree holds at every level of the tree. DINNERS is a key that comes before DISHES but follows BOAT.

The alphabetic order of a database tree makes it possible to "divide-and-conquer" when searching for a specific key. Suppose that we look for DISHES using the database tree of Fig. 4.9. We begin at the HEADER of

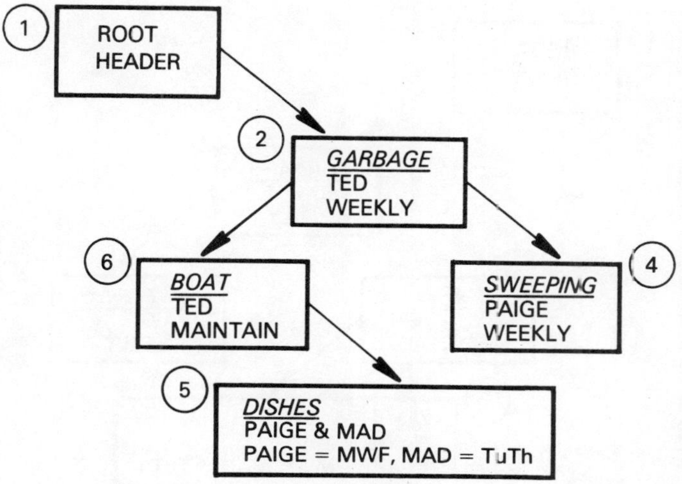

Fig. 4.10 Database tree after deleting "Dinners" key

the tree. The HEADER is stored at record zero of the disk file. It contains two *pointers*, L and R (for left and right). The L pointer is not used, so we follow the R pointer to record 2, which contains GARBAGE.

READ #1 %L*S+H, J$, A$, B$, C$, L, R

This READ causes direct access to a record beginning at location L*S+H of the file:

L = record number
S = length (in characters) of each record
H = length (in characters) of HEADER record

We continue our search for K$ = DISHES by going down the left (L) branch of the tree to DINNERS. We elected to take the L pointer rather than the R pointer given in GARBAGE because DISHES is "less than" GARBAGE in terms of alphabetical order.

Again, comparing DISHES to DINNERS produces a new path to follow from the third record. Since DISHES is "greater than" DINNERS, we follow the R pointer to record 5.

Finally, the search for DISHES stops. We have found the matching key in three comparisons and three records instead of five. In short, we have searched the disk file without looking at every record stored.

The database tree must be kept in order even though records are removed or inserted. The result of removing the DINNERS record, for example, will produce a tree as shown in Fig. 4.10. We replace a deletion record with its left subrecord. Since the left subrecord may also have subrecords, we must be careful to attach the DISHES record to the BOAT record by searching for the rightmost subrecord of BOAT (which is

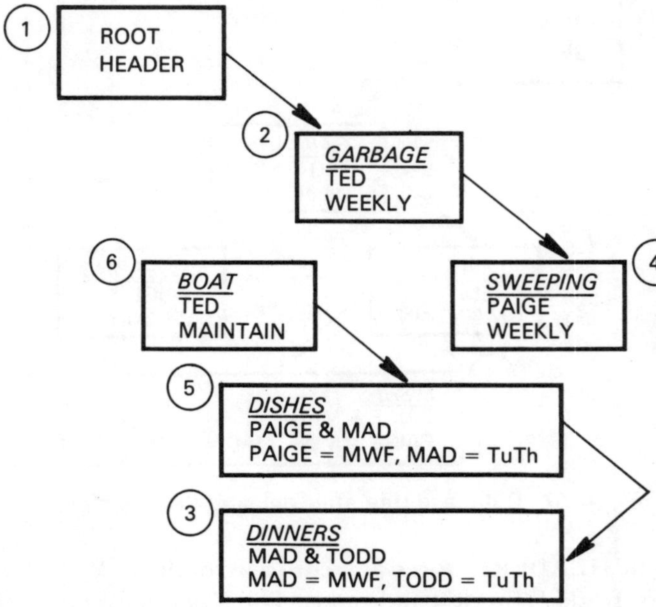

Fig. 4.11 Reinstatement of "Dinners" to database tree

empty in this example) and then attaching DISHES to that rightmost record.

New records must be added in a way that does not disturb the order of the database tree. Figure 4.11 shows what happens when we reinstate DINNERS to the tree of Fig. 4.10. Since BOAT now occupies the position of left subrecord to GARBAGE, DINNERS must be inserted (in order) below BOAT.

The database tree, its corresponding routines, and file space (called CHORES) require care in constructing. A set of programs for this application is shown in Fig. 4.12.

Note the method used to allocate disk space. A *bit vector* is a string of ones and zeros, as shown by F$ in the programs. If the A1th character of F$ is set to "1", the A1th record of the file is allocated to the database tree. If F$(A1) is zero, we may use that record to place a new entry into the tree. In the version of BASIC being used, F$(I, J) means to extract from F$ the string beginning at character position I and ending at character position J.

The allocation and free routines operate on F$ to yield records when needed and to return records to F$ when they are deleted from the CHORES file.

The initialization routine establishes a file information record. This record saves the value of F$, the file name, and the lengths S and H. Initialization is done once, only, for each application.

```
LOAD CHORLIST
READY
LIST
100 REM*********************************************
110 REM
120 REM      MENU PROGRAM FOR RETRIEVAL
130 REM
140 REM*********************************************
150 REM
155 LET M=20 : REM -----MAX. SIZE OF F
160 DIM F$(20),P$(8),Q$(8),A$(20),B$(20),C$(20),D$(20),J$(12),K$(12)
165 INPUT"ENTER PASSWORD( 8 CHAR ):",P$
170 PRINT"SELECT ONE OF THE FOLLOWING :"
175 PRINT
180 PRINT"     1. INITIALIZE THE DATABASE"
185 PRINT"     2. BUILD (INPUT) THE DATABASE"
190 PRINT"     3. DISPLAY AN ITEM FROM DATABASE"
195 PRINT"     4. DELETE AN ITEM FROM DATABASE"
200 PRINT"     5. STOP."
210 INPUT"ENTER NUMBER SELECTED :",N
220 IF N>5 THEN 170
225 IF N<1 THEN 170
230 REM
235 REM------------EXECUTE THE SELECTED ROUTINE-------------
240 REM
250 ON N GOTO 251,252,253,254,298
251 GOSUB 1000 : GOTO 270
252 GOSUB 2000 : GOTO 270
253 GOSUB 3000 : GOTO 270
254 GOSUB 4000 : GOTO 270
260 REM
270 CLOSE #1
275 OPEN #1,P$
280 WRITE #1 %0,P$,F$,S,H
290 CLOSE #1
295 GOTO 170
296 REM--------------REPEAT MENU-----------------------
298 CLOSE #1
299 END
300 REM**********************************************
310 REM
320 REM          ALLOCATE SPACE
330 REM
340 REM**********************************************
350 IF F$(M,M)="1" THEN 355 ELSE 365
355 PRINT"DISK FULL"
360 LET A1=0 : RETURN
361 REM
365 FOR I=1 TO  M
370 IF  F$(I,I)="1" THEN 385 ELSE 375
375 LET A1=I
380 EXIT 390
385 NEXT I
390 LET F$(A1,A1)="1" : RETURN
400 REM**********************************************
410 REM
```

Fig. 4.12 Menu program

```
420 REM         FREE SPACE
430 REM
440 REM*************************************************
450 REM
460 LET F$(A1,A1)="0"
465 PRINT"RECORD ",A1," DELETED"
470 RETURN
600 REM*************************************************
601 REM
602 REM       SEARCH DATABASE TREE
603 REM
604 REM*************************************************
605 REM
606 REM       A2 IS TERMINAL NODE OF TREE AFTER SEARCH
607 REM       A4 IS 0 IF "NOT FOUND", A4=A2 IF "FOUND"
608 REM       A3 IS POINTER TO NODE BEFORE A2
609 REM
610 REM------REPEAT UNTIL TERMINAL NODE FOUND-----------
611 REM
620 LET A4=1 : LET A2=0
630 FOR I=1 TO M
640  READ #1 %A4*S+H,J$,C$,D$,L,R
650  LET A3=A2 : LET A2=A4
655  REM
656  REM-----DOES IT MATCH, IF SO, "FOUND"------------
657  REM
660    IF J$=K$ THEN 735
670    IF J$<K$ THEN 680 ELSE 700
680  LET G=1 : LET A4=R
690  GOTO 720
695  REM
696  REM-----ELSE, LEFT SUBTREE----------------------
698  REM
700  LET G=0 : LET A4=L
710  REM-----END OF IF-THEN-ELSE-----------------------
720  IF A4=0 THEN 735
730 NEXT I
735 REM
740 RETURN
1000 REM*************************************************
1001 REM
1002 REM         INITIALIZE DATABASE
1003 REM
1004 REM*************************************************
1005 REM
1010 OPEN #1,P$
1015 REM
1016 REM---------GET RECORD SIZE-------------------------
1017 REM
1020 INPUT"ENTER RECORD LENGTH IN CHARACTERS :",S
1025 IF S>255 THEN 1020
1030 INPUT"ENTER HEADER LENGTH IN CHARACTERS :",H
1035 IF H>255 THEN 1030
1040 REM
1041 REM---------INITIALIZE ALLOCATION TABLE-------------
1042 REM
```

Fig. 4.12 Menu program (cont'd)

```
1045 LET F$(1,1)="1"
1050 FOR I=2 TO M
1055  LET F$(I)="0"
1060 NEXT I
1070 REM
1075 REM---------WRITE ROOT OF TREE----------------------
1079 REM
1080 LET J$="%$#?!&!#$%&$" : C$="HEADER RECORD" : D$="SEARCH TREE"
1090 WRITE #1 %S+H,J$,C$,D$,0,0
1100 RETURN
1120 REM
2000 REM**************************************************
2001 REM
2002 REM          BUILD DATABASE
2003 REM
2004 REM**************************************************
2005 REM
2010 OPEN #1,P$
2020 READ #1 %0,Q$,F$,S,H
2030 IF P$=Q$ THEN 2060 : REM - - - - - - - - - - - - - :
2040 PRINT"WRONG PASSWORD !"                             :
2050 RETURN                                              :
2055 REM                                                 :
2060 INPUT"ENTER CHORE (12 CHAR. MAX.) :",K$
2070 IF K$="" THEN RETURN : REM<************************
2075 REM
2080 INPUT"ENTER SLAVE'S NAME (20 CHAR. MAX.) :",A$
2090 INPUT"ENTER COMMENT (20 CHAR. MAX.) :",B$
2100 REM
2105 REM---------IS THIS THE FIRST ENTRY ?--------------
2106 REM
2110 IF F$(1,1)="0" THEN 2120 ELSE 2200
2120 LET F$(1,1)="1"
2130 REM
2134 REM---------YES, INSERT NEW RECORD------------------
2136 REM
2140 WRITE #1 %S+H,K$,A$,B$,L,R
2150 GOTO 2060
2160 REM
2170 REM---------NO, LOOK FOR A PLACE IN THE TREE---------
2180 REM
2200 GOSUB 600
2210 REM
2220 IF A4=0 THEN 2274
2260 PRINT"RECORD EXISTS ALREADY!!!"
2270 GOTO 2060
2271 REM
2272 REM------------GET DISK SPACE---------------------
2273 REM
2274 GOSUB 300
2275 REM
2276 REM-----------UPDATE POINTER TO NEW ENTRY--------------
2277 REM
2280 READ #1 %A2*S+H,J$,C$,D$,L,R
2285 REM
2290 IF G=0 THEN L=A1 ELSE R=A1
2300 WRITE #1 %A2*S+H,J$,C$,D$,L,R
```

Fig. 4.12 Menu program (cont'd)

```
2310 WRITE #1 %A1*S+H,K$,A$,B$,0,0
2320 GOTO 2060
2400 REM
2405 REM-------------NEW RECORD INSERTED INTO DATABASE------
2406 REM
2500 RETURN
2510 REM
3000 REM*******************************************************
3001 REM
3002 REM                 DISPLAY A RECORD
3003 REM
3004 REM*******************************************************
3005 REM
3010 OPEN #1,P$
3015 READ #1 %0,Q$,F$,S,H
3016 IF P$=Q$ THEN 3020
3017 PRINT"WRONG PASSWORD !!!"
3018 RETURN    :   REM<************************************
3019 REM
3020 INPUT"ENTER KEY (CHORE) :",K$
3030 IF K$="" THEN RETURN : REM<***************************
3040 REM
3041 REM-------------LOOKUP KEY IN TREE--------------------
3042 REM
3050 GOSUB 600
3055 IF A4=0 THEN 3100
3056 REM
3057 REM--------------RECORD FOUND ! ----------------------
3058 REM
3060 PRINT"CHORE :",J$
3061 PRINT"SLAVE :",C$
3062 PRINT"COMMENTS :",D$
3070 REM
3071 REM-------------DO YOU WANT TO REPEAT ?---------------
3072 REM
3080 GOTO 3020
3085 REM
3090 REM-------------BAD ENTRY----------------------------
3095 REM
3100 PRINT"ENTRY WITH THAT KEY DOESN'T EXIST"
3110 GOTO 3020
3115 REM
3201 REM
4000 REM*******************************************************
4001 REM
4002 REM           DELETE A RECORD
4003 REM
4004 REM*******************************************************
4050 REM
4055 OPEN #1,P$
4056 READ #1 %0,Q$,F$,S,H
4060 INPUT"ENTER CHORE TO BE DELETED :",K$
4070 IF K$="" THEN RETURN : REM<***************************
4080 REM
4085 REM---------LOOKUP RECORD----------------------------
4090 REM
```

Fig. 4.12 Menu program (cont'd)

```
4100      GOSUB 600
4110 REM
4120 IF A4=0 THEN PRINT"ENTRY NOT FOUND."
4121 IF A4=0 THEN 4060
4125 REM
4126 REM---------FOUND---------------------------------------
4127 REM
4130 INPUT"ARE YOU SURE ?",Q$
4140 IF Q$="YES" THEN 4200
4150 PRINT"I DIDN'T THINK SO !!"
4160 GOTO 4060
4170 REM
4171 REM---------DELETE THE RECORD-----------------------
4172 REM
4200 READ #1 %A2*S+H,J$,C$,D$,L1,R1
4215 READ #1 %A3*S+H,J$,C$,D$,L,R
4216 IF G=0 THEN L=L1 ELSE R=L1
4220 WRITE #1 %A3*S+H,J$,C$,D$,L,R
4240 REM
4241 REM--------FREE DISK SPACE---------------------------
4242 REM
4250 LET A1=A2
4270     GOSUB 400
4275 REM
4280 REM---------LOOKUP PLACE TO INSERT R1----------------
4285 REM
4290      GOSUB 600
4295 REM
4300 READ #1 %A2*S+H,J$,C$,D$,L,R
4310 WRITE #1 %A2*S+H,J$,C$,D$,L,R1
4320 REM
4330 GOTO 4060
4340 REM
9999 REM
```

Fig. 4.12 Menu program (cont'd)

The look-up routine searches the file using the database tree search described earlier. We stop the search when the search key (K$) equals the stored record key (J$).

Careful study of these programs can reveal many useful programming tips that may be used in future projects.

4.3 A Shopping List

Roger and Mable were very pleased with their chore list program. They decided that it would also be helpful to make up a shopping list that would be added to during the week and then used on Friday for shopping.

Their shopping list contains the names of the items needed, the quantity (loaf, can, 12-oz. package, etc.), and the names of the person who requested them. In other words, the list is quite similar to the chore list.

Each new entry in the shopping list must be checked to make sure that it does not already exist there. The program must therefore search the database tree before inserting the new item in the list.

The database tree programs of Figure 4.12 search the tree to locate an available space. The new item will not be added to the tree unless there are no matching (conflicting) keys. Thus, we can use the database tree to construct shopping lists.

Roger and Mable modified their chore chart to handle shopping lists. They initialized the database tree with different values (68 and 56, respectively) and made minor modifications to their programs to reflect the differences between shopping lists and chore charts.

The point illustrated by Roger and Mable is that the database tree is general. It can be used in a variety of applications, all of which satisfy information retrieval conditions:

1. Rapid lookup
2. Ability to add new items at any time
3. Ability to delete old items at any time
4. Ability to change an entry rapidly at any time

Both Roger and Mable were pleased with their intelligent cupboards, smart stove, and witty refrigerator. They lived happily for a while.

Chapter Five

THE BEDROOM (WORD/TEXT PROCESSING)

"Harold, I'm warning you. If you bring that . . . that . . THING into our bedroom, I'll go to mother's! Harold, do you hear me? Harold! HAROLD!"

Man's finest hour, midnight, July 12, 1978

Harold and Ariel were married for 15 years before they had their first argument. Then, all hell seemed to break loose when Harold became consumed by his personal computer.

Luckily, the two of them came to me before it was too late. I had just finished installing a microminiature CB radio in the T-shirt of our neighbor's eight-year-old when the doorbell rang.

"Oh, I'm sorry to bother you at home," Ariel blurted. Harold stood next to her, looking down at his feet. Ariel was a small red-haired woman of about 40. They looked so pitiful, I asked them to step inside, even though I had little time to analyze their problem.

"Come in, I'll be right with you," I said in a solemn tone and left them to attend to the boy. "Jimmy, are you sure you know how to wear your CB shirt, now?"

"Yes, I know what to do. When mom and dad want me for supper, ya know, or sumpin' else, they'll call me on my T-shirt." He beamed with pride and ran out into the late afternoon dusk.

Harold and Ariel were sitting on the sofa, glaring at each other, when I returned to listen to their story.

"Ah reckon Ary has a rightéous cause for concern," Harold drawled. "She 'n I been tugether for nigh on 15 years, and this here is the first mean argument we've had." He was still sheepishly looking down at his shoes.

"Well, Ariel, what do you have to say about this?" I wasn't sure what their problem was.

"Harold got a personal computer and is spending lots of time with it. In fact, he spends more time with it than with me."

"Yes, that is a common problem in our society today." I tried to sympathize.

"Well, that wasn't so bad, until last night. I called for Harold to come to bed at about midnight. He said he was on his way. I'd bought a new gown. . . ."

"Ya, one of them thin kind." Harold couldn't keep himself from interrupting.

"Well, ah, it wasn't . . . shut up, Harold!" Ariel was blushing.

"Go on, Ariel, I don't mind, just relax," I assured her.

"Anyway, I put on my gown and waited for Harold to come to bed. Then, here he came, luggin' that damn computer into *my* bedroom!" Ariel became flushed, again, only this time it was with real anger.

I knew then that my work was cut out for me, as Harold would say. But I assured them both that their marriage could be saved, and the computer, too.

After several months of therapy, Harold, Ariel, and the computer lived happily ever after. The solution was obvious:

Harold took my advice and together we developed the programs in this chapter. The first program generates four-letter words. Four-letter words happen to be one of Ariel's fetishes but more important, we were able to improve this program so that it would generate entire sentences. In fact, the personal computer in Harold and Ariel's bedroom "learned" to write X-rated poetry, once a list of words had been entered into its memory.

Finally, we were able to program Harold's personal computer to listen to Ariel (something Harold hates to do). Ariel can tell the computer what to do, and the computer says things like, "Yes, Ariel," "Thank you, Ariel," and "You are right as usual, Ariel."

The end of this story is a happy one. Ariel spends most of the day talking to Harold's personal computer while Harold is at work. In the evening, Harold and Ariel put soft music on the stereo, turn the lights down low, and listen to poetry from their personal computer.

The following sections describe how Harold programmed his personal computer so that it would entrance Ariel, save his marriage, and "understand" simple English.

5.1 Four-Letter Words

We will now see how a computer may be programmed to produce unexpected output by designing a four-letter word generator. The resultant output of such a program often surprises even the designer.

Suppose that we want to produce a PG-rated program for randomly generating N four-letter words. The program that does this must store vowels and consonants in separate string arrays in BASIC. The program then begins generating a word by randomly selecting either a vowel or consonant, concatenating the newly selected letter to the word, and storing the word as a string.

The BASIC functions used to manipulate strings are given below. They exist in different forms in other dialects of BASIC but serve the same purpose.

Concatenation (+ or &)

The concatenation operator joins two strings together to form a single string. Suppose that C$ contains a single letter of the alphabet, and W$ is a partially constructed word:

```
W$ = W$ & C$
```

This assignment statement (or its equivalent in another dialect of BASIC) produces a longer word, W$, which now includes the letter C$ at its end.

Separation (SEG or –)

The opposite of concatenation is separation. Suppose that we want to extract the substring of length 1, position J, from string A$:

```
C$ = SEG(A$, J, 1)
```

This assignment copies a single letter from position J of A$ into C$.

Since many four-letter words are uninteresting, we may want to produce words according to a few rules. Spelling rules are generally part of a language. For example, in English, the letter "u" follows the letter "q" in almost every case.

A model of spelling rules may be constructed by observing how English letters are put together to form words. Suppose that we enforce the following rules in generating four-letter words:

1. Every word begins with a consonant.
2. The second letter is always a vowel.
3. The third and fourth letters are vowels 50 percent of the time and consonants 50 percent of the time.

```
100 REM==================================
110 REM
120 REM      GRAFFITO (4-LETTER WORDS)
130 REM
140 REM----------------------------------
150 DIM A$(5),B$(20),W$(4),C$(1)
160 LET W$=""
170 REM
180 REM---STORE ALPHABET ----------------
190 LET A$="AEIOU"
200 LET B$="BCDFGHJKLMNPRSTVW"
210 REM
220 REM---HOW MANY 4-LETTER WORDS--------
230 REM
240 PRINT "HOW MANY WORDS DO YOU WANT?";
250 INPUT N
260 FOR N=N TO 1 STEP -1
270 REM
280 REM
290 REM---SELECT RANDOM CONSONANT-------
300 LET J=INT(17*RND(1)+1)
310 LET C$=SEG(B$,J,1)
320 LET W$=W$&C$
330 REM
340 REM---SELECT RANDOM VOWEL-----------
350 LET J=INT(5*RND(1)+1)
360 LET C$=SEG(A$,J,1)
370 LET W$=W$&C$
380 REM
390 REM---SELECT VOWEL OR CONSONANT-----
400 FOR I=1 TO 2
410 IF RND(1)<0.5 THEN 470
420 LET J=INT(17*RND(1)+1)
430 LET C$=SEG(B$,J,1)
440 LET W$=W$&C$
450 GO TO 500
460 REM---GET A VOWEL--------------------
470 LET J=INT(5*RND(1)+1)
480 LET C$=SEG(A$,J,1)
490 LET W$=W$&C$
500 NEXT I
510 REM
520 REM
530 PRINT W$
540 LET W$=""
550 NEXT N
560 REM
570 END
```

Fig. 5.1 Program Graffito

4. The third and fourth letters are selected independently of one another.

Program GRAFFITO (see Fig. 5.1) generates four-letter words according to the rules above. It uses the string functions described earlier and will generate as many four-letter words as requested. A sample of the words produced by GRAFFITO is given below:

FIBL	WUCC
JIBE	MEOU
TERC	SEET
CUOC	LURE

Clearly, the rules given in GRAFFITO lack enough structure to make the four-letter words interesting. Yet, every so often in a long run, the result is a four-letter word deserving to be banned in Boston.

5.2 The Poetry Robot

Since the beginning of the electronic digital computer era, computer hobbyists have tried to program machines to understand natural language. In fact, very early in the history of computing, a group of scientists calling themselves *computational linguists* were confident that in the near future machines would be able to recognize English. Unfortunately, their goal has never been fully achieved because of the startling realization that English is more complicated than thought at first glance. Progress, however elusive, has been made, and the purpose of this section is to demonstrate how to use existing techniques to build your own English-sentence-generating programs.

Baby Computers

Electronic computers don't think, nor are they subject to evolution and natural selection as human beings are, but it may be possible to simulate thought, and furthermore, to simulate evolution with a computer. If we can discover the laws of thought, and if we can breed a race of computers that get "smarter" in every succeeding generation, then wouldn't it be possible to develop machines that "think" like human beings? This is the idea that motivated psycholinguists to study how infants learn to speak.

To understand how language works requires a knowledge of two things: (1) syntax, and (2) semantics. Syntax deals with how words are put together to form "correct" sentences. For example, we know from experience that "house, the red, over the hill big" is syntactically incorrect; what is meant, of course, is "the red house over the big hill." Thus, while we are able to discover the meaning of the garbled phrase, the order of the words violates English grammar.

Syntax governs the grammar of a language, but semantics governs the meaning of a sentence. In either case, we are concerned with the unambiguous use of English by a robot. Whenever the syntax is garbled or the words are poorly chosen, a sentence invariably becomes more difficult to understand. In such cases we say the sentence is *ambiguous*. Remember this word, because it plays an important part in the process of making a computer understand English.

In some cases it is possible for an English sentence to be ambiguous in another sense. For instance, "the sharp corners on the round table . . .", is syntactically correct but meaningless. We easily dismiss this phrase as gibberish, but a machine can recognize absurdity only by means of well-defined rules of meaning.

We know that every sentence constructed by human beings or machines obeys certain rules. In fact, we learn the rules of grammar in grade school. We are taught to diagram sentences. We learn that sentences have subject and verb phrases. Subject phrases usually consist of a noun or two and an occasional adjective. Verb phrases consist of verbs, adverbs, and often direct and indirect objects. Unfortunately, since the lessons frequently fail to take hold, the English language is frequently abused.

The point is that sentences are formed according to rules learned in childhood. But how do we learn to speak?

Scientists have studied the grammar of infants all over the world searching for an answer to this question. Amazingly, they discovered an important fact: all children of the world begin speaking using the *same* grammar! Perhaps the basic grammar is inborn; perhaps it is learned. We don't know, but the fact is that every child uses the same set of rules regardless of where he or she is born, what language his or her parents speak, and regardless of his or her color, religion, or sex.

The only difference between Swahili and English at the age of 18 months is the set of *tokens* used in each language. Tokens are the actual words (spoken or written) used in expressing meaning. In Swahili, we might say "me-me" instead of "I," but the grammar is the same in both languages *up to the age of about 18 months.*

A collection of tokens (words) forms a vocabulary that we shall call V_T:

$$V_T = (\text{shoe, hot, milk})$$

In this example, V_T consists of single words of English. These words are put together in English (or their equivalents in French, Swahili, German, etc.) using the grammar of single words by all children of age 18 months or less. We give the rule as follows:

$$\text{Sentence} = \text{word, where word is from } V_T$$

We say that the sentence of an infant is constructed by selecting a word from the vocabulary V_T.

Linguists conjecture that the words in V_T were invented by cavemen while arguing with cavewomen. In one culture, "Ugh!" may have meant,

"You are the sweetest of them all," whereas in another culture it may have been rewarded with a clubbing. Why women are like this has always baffled men, and even to this day, linguists cannot explain women or the origins of words.

Clearly, language would be an uninteresting waste of time if it consisted solely of single-word sentences. At the age of 18 months or so, most infants develop a two-word grammar consisting of two kinds of words. The *open words* are tokens that are taken from the list of single words:

Open words = (shoe, hot, milk)

Pivotal words are added to V_T; for example,

Pivotal words = (my, green)

The grammar dictates that an infant select words from V_T made from the open and pivotal words, as follows:

Sentence = open word + open word

or

Sentence = pivotal word + open word

In other words, the sentence structure (syntax) of an 18-month-old child in Africa, China, or England consists of either two open words or one pivotal word followed by one open word. All other possible combinations are avoided.

If we assume a child with the vocabulary of V_T = ((open words), (pivotal words)), then the following examples of speech are possible:

Sentence = open word + open word
= "milk" + "hot"
= "milk hot"

Another possible sentence that a baby could express is derived in the same way, but with different words.

Sentence = pivotal word + open word
= "my" + "milk"
= "my milk"

Since a baby cannot put two pivotal words together in one sentence, it would not be possible for him or her to say "green my." We can see why this is against the rules:

"green my" = pivotal word + pivotal word
Sentence ≠ pivotal word + pivotal word

After mastering this simple grammar, children of the world rapidly advance to a grammar that allows four kinds of sentences:

Sentence = open word
or, open word + open word
or, open word + pivotal word
or, pivotal word + open word

At about the age of three years, the influence of culture begins to affect the innate ability of children to form sentences.

When a child begins using three words in a sentence, he learns to form them according to the rules of his native language. Indeed, the differences among French, English, Swahili, and all other languages of the world begin to appear at this stage of child development.

Computers As Syntax Mechanics

In a sense, we may view human beings as syntax mechanics. We take in sentences, modify, dissect, repair, or in some manner digest the syntactic structure and invest it with meaning. The sentence, "The girl kissed the horse," immediately generates envy for the horse when we *parse* the sentence and realize (through a picture in our mind, perhaps) what the sentence means. Hence, we *parse* or "recognize" the sentence in both syntactic and semantic senses.

In order to program a computer to parse a sentence of English, we must create an artificial sentence diagram called the phrase-marker. A phrase-marker for "The girl kissed the horse" is shown below.

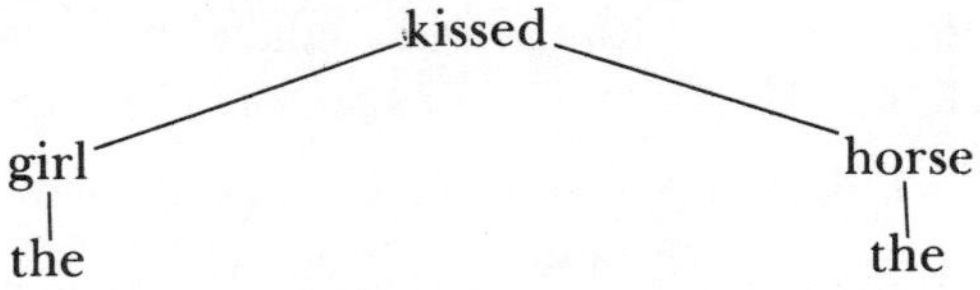

If we had recognized (parsed) the modified sentence, "The beautiful girl kissed the ugly horse," or, "The ugly girl kissed the beautiful horse," we would get two different phrase-markers, as shown below:

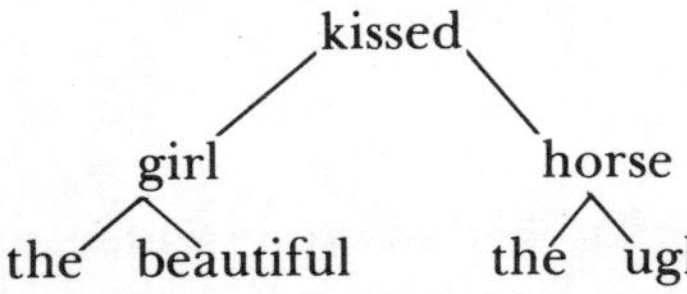

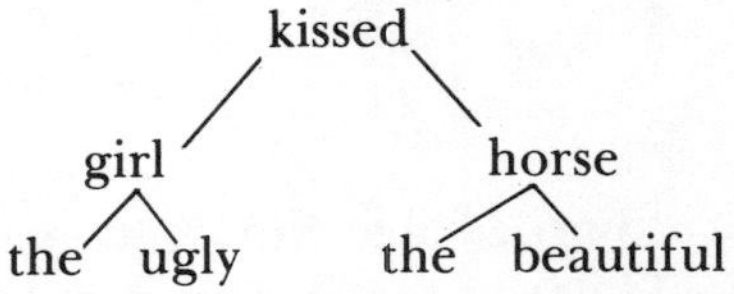

In the phrase-markers above, we have little trouble deciding which of the two actors is beautiful and which is ugly. Thus, the phrase-markers are clearly unique, and we say that they are *unambiguous*.

Consider now the ambiguous sentence, "The man drove a truck full of beer." The two possible phrase-markers for this sentence are shown below:

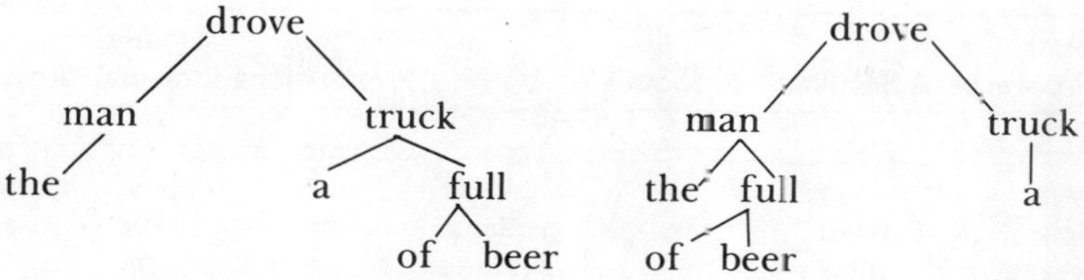

Since we cannot determine which phrase-marker is "correct," the sentence cannot be parsed into a unique phrase-marker. Hence, it is an ambiguous sentence.

How can we expect a computer to understand ambiguous sentences if we cannot understand them ourselves? Obviously, we are accustomed to guessing, using context, and adjusting to cultural biases in order to clarify the meaning of a sentence. We know for example that "George kicked the bucket last night" means that George died rather than actually attempted a field goal with a bucket. In short, we must provide a computer with the rules of semantics before it can understand language as well as we do.

The Computer As Poet (Even If It Doesn't Know It)

We must know the rules of grammar and the rules of meaning before we can program a computer to understand English. Although the rules of English grammar are well formulated, the rules of English semantics are more difficult to discover. Let us see what can be done with the easy part of the problem first before tackling the more difficult problem of meaning.

Suppose that we have a robot computer capable of "speaking." Somehow the words of a sentence are converted into sound, and the sound is broadcast through a speaker system. The details of the formation of the robot's "voice" will be ignored for now, and instead, we will concentrate on the rules of English necessary to form sentences.

To mechanically produce grammatically correct sentences, we need a computer model of grammar. Recall that grammar governs the placement of words in sentences. We need both a grammar and a vocabulary in order to begin.

As an illustration, the vocabulary of Figure 5.2 is input to a program that writes English poetry. Each line of poetry may consist of nouns, adjectives, pronouns, verbs, prepositions, and articles. The poetry, as can be seen, is romantic and involves a set of rhyming objects. We can program a computer to produce "original" poetry from this limited vocabulary by using a phrase-marker model of grammar.

We use the phrase-marker model of sentences to produce sentences that are "legal" in terms of the romantic poetry to be produced. This

Nouns (subject phrase)	Adjectives	Pronouns	Verbs	Prepositions	Nouns (objects)	Articles
1	2	3	4	5	6	7
eyes	hot	your	glow	under	pie	the
lips	lewd		radiate	in	sky	a
caresses	blue		explode	on	thigh	
love's	red			near	sigh	
				from		

Fig. 5.2 Vocabulary of poetry program

model is expressed in a notation exactly like the notation used to describe baby talk. The set of grammar rules in this case is called a *generative production* system.

Grammar of Poetry System

Sentence = noun phrase + verb phrase
Noun phrase = pronoun + noun
    or, pronoun + adjective + noun
    or, noun (possessive case) + adjective + noun
Verb phrase = verb
    or, verb + prepositional phrase
Prepositional phrase = preposition + article + object
    or, preposition + article + adjective + object

These four simple rules are all that we need to produce "intelligible" poetry. Another way to view this model is given by the diagram of Fig. 5.3. The diagram is useful in writing the computer program because it shows how to produce each word in each line of poetry. Beginning at START, we follow the arrow to the NOUN PHRASE. The NOUN PHRASE leads to a PRONOUN which, in turn, leads to a NOUN in 20 percent of the sentences and to an ADJECTIVE in 80 percent of the sentences. Every ADJECTIVE is followed by a NOUN and every NOUN is followed by a VERB PHRASE. Thus, we can generate lines of poetry, each line different from the others, by traversing the arrows in the model of Fig. 5.3.

The BASIC programs of Fig. 5.4 perform the path traversal exactly as we have illustrated. These programs were run on a system with a random number generator to produce random selection of words from the vocabulary and random path selection.

Each poem consists of a number of sentences indicated by an input value. The words are eight characters long (blank padding) and are stored in a string array, V$. The vector V of eight elements contains the subscripts of V$ corresponding to the beginning of the list of nouns, adjectives, etc., within V$. Thus, S is the value of the subscript of the beginning of each list.

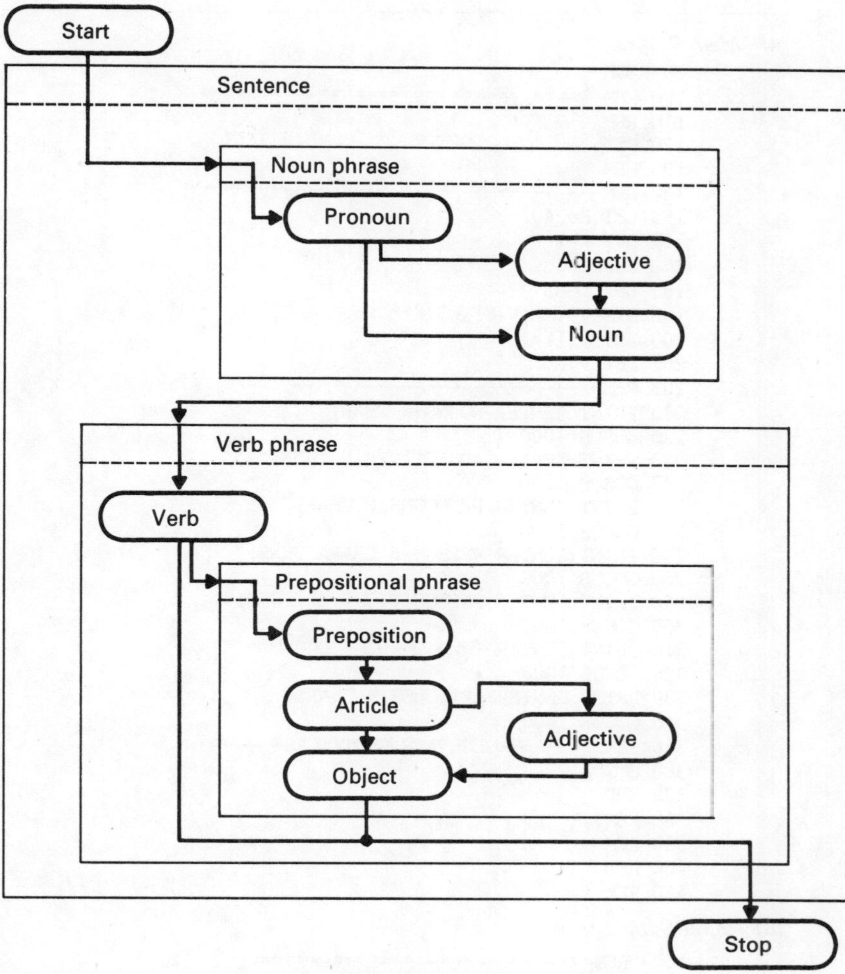

Fig. 5.3 The grammar of poetry

Since we have assumed a robot capable of speaking simple words, the program of Fig. 5.4 is used to produce the words one at a time. Of course, we would need a voice-response unit to make the actual sound. Instead, the program prints the words rather than speaking them.

A sample of a dozen sentences of amateur poetry is shown in Fig. 5.5. Clearly, this poetry is passionate enough to be classified as the first X-rated output from a robot!

The generative model presented above avoids the problem of ambiguity illustrated earlier because it is originated by the robot rather than a human being. The robot obeys rigid rules specified in the program, whereas human beings break the same rules all too frequently. In order to make a robot "understand" the same poetry that it generates would require a much more sophisticated program.

(A) Main Program

```
10 PAGE
100 REM ==================================
110 REM
120 REM          POETRY
130 REM
140 REM----------------------------------
150 LET M=240
160 LET K=1
170 LET S=1
180 LET L=8
190 DIM V$(M),V(8),W$(8)
200 LET V(1)=1
201 LET V$=""
205 REM------------------------------
210 PRINT "ENTER NOUNS(8 CHAR)"
220 GOSUB 1000
230 PRINT "ENTER ADJECTIVES(8 CHAR)"
240 GOSUB 1000
250 PRINT "ENTER PRONOUNS(8 CHAR)"
260 GOSUB 1000
270 PRINT "ENTER VERBS (8 CHARACTERS)"
280 GOSUB 1000
290 PRINT "ENTER PREPOSITIONS (8 CHAR)"
300 GOSUB 1000
310 PRINT "ENTER OBJECTS (8 CHAR)"
320 GOSUB 1000
330 PRINT "ENTER ARTICLES(8 CHAR)"
340 GOSUB 1000
350 REM --------GENERATE SENTENCES-------
360 GOSUB 2000
370 END
380 REM
390 REM
400 REM
410 REM
```

(B) Input Subprogram

```
1000 REM==============================
1010 REM
1020 REM        INPUT VOCABULARY
1030 REM
1040 REM-----------------------------
1045 LET S=S+1
1050 REM---REPEAT LOOP --------------
1060 PRINT "WORD=";
1070 INPUT W$
1075 IF W$="" THEN 1230
1080 REM---PACK WORD INTO VOCABULARY--
1110 LET V$=V$&W$
1111 FOR I=LEN(W$)+1 TO L
1112 LET V$=V$&" "
1113 NEXT I
1120 REM---MARK BEGINNING OF UNIT ----
1130 LET V(S)=K+L
1140 LET K=K+L
1150 IF K<M THEN 1050
1160 PRINT "VOCABULARY FULL"
1230 RETURN
```

Fig. 5.4 Poetry program

(C) Sentence Generator

```
2000 REM==============================
2010 REM
2020 REM        GENERATE SENTENCES
2030 REM
2040 REM------------------------------
2050 PRINT "ENTER NUMBER OF SENTENCES YOU WANT=";
2060 INPUT N
2070 FOR N=N TO 1 STEP -1
2080 REM---NOUN PHRASE----------------
2090 GOSUB 3000
2100 REM---VERB PHRASE----------------
2110 GOSUB 4000
2120 PRINT
2130 NEXT N
2140 RETURN
2150 REM------------------------------
```

(D) Noun Phrase Generator

```
3000 REM==============================
3010 REM
3020 REM       NOUN PHRASE
3030 REM
3040 REM------------------------------
3050 LET S=3
3060 REM---GET PRONOUN----------------
3070 GOSUB 5000
3080 IF RND(1)<0.2 THEN 3500
3090 LET S=2
3100 REM---GET ADJECTIVE--------------
3110 GOSUB 5000
3120 REM---GET NOUN-------------------
3500 LET S=1
3510 GOSUB 5000
3520 RETURN
```

(E) Verb Phrase Generator

```
4000 REM==============================
4010 REM
4020 REM       VERB PHRASE
4030 REM
4040 REM------------------------------
4050 LET S=4
4055 REM---GET VERB-------------------
4060 GOSUB 5000
4070 IF RND(1)<0.1 THEN 4500
4080 LET S=5
4090 REM---GET PREPOSITION------------
4100 GOSUB 5000
4110 LET S=7
4120 REM---GET ARTICLE----------------
4130 GOSUB 5000
4140 IF RND(1)<0.3 THEN 4400
4150 LET S=2
4160 REM---GET ADJECTIVE--------------
4170 GOSUB 5000
4400 REM---GET OBJECT-----------------
4410 LET S=6
4420 GOSUB 5000
4500 RETURN
```

Fig. 5.4 Poetry program (cont'd)

(F) Output of a Word at a Time

```
5000 REM==============================
5010 REM
5020 REM        PRINT THE WORD
5030 REM
5040 REM------------------------------
5050 LET N1=(V(S+1)-V(S))/L
5060 LET N1=INT(RND(1)*N1)
5070 LET W$=SEG(V$,V(S)+N1*L,L)
5080 PRINT W$;
5090 RETURN
```

Fig. 5.4 Poetry program (cont'd)

```
LOVE'S  BLUE   CARESSES GLOW    FROM    A      LEWD   THIGH
YOUR    HOT    LIPS     GLOW    ON      A      LEWD   SIGH
YOUR    LEWD   EYES     EXPLODE FROM    THE    BLUE   THIGH
YOUR    HOT    CARESSES EXPLODE UNDER   THE    RED    SIGH
YOUR    RED    CARESSES GLOW    ON      A      RED    SKY
YOUR    BLUE   LIPS     RADIATE UNDER   THE    RED    THIGH
YOUR   EYES     RADIATE ON      THE     BLUE   THIGH
YOUR    BLUE   EYES     RADIATE ON      A      SKY
YOUR   LIPS     EXPLODE NEAR    THE     SIGH
LOVE'S  RED    CARESSES GLOW    FROM    THE    RED    SKY
YOUR    HOT    EYES     RADIATE
LOVE'S  RED    CARESSES RADIATE IN      A      HOT    PIE
```

Fig. 5.5 Poetry from the robot poet

The Meaning of Meaning

Actually, what we expect of the robot is more than we expect of ourselves. We must understand the meaning of meaning itself before the robot can be programmed to accept English as an input.

Suppose that we use the robot's "ear" to input a sentence such as, "Robot, come here." Also, assume that the robot is sophisticated enough to be able to match the spoken sound patterns of our voice against a stored "library" of sound patterns and determine that we have spoken either, "Robot, come hear," or, "Robot, come here." The robot now has the task of parsing this phrase and storing it in a phrase-marker. Two possible markers are:

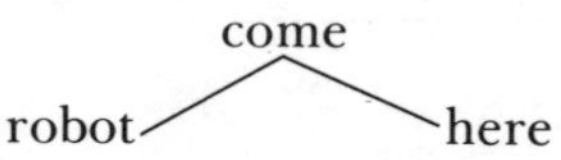

(A)

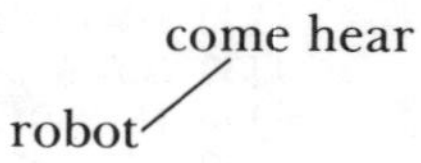

(B)

In case (A) above, the robot interprets our command as a directive to move closer, whereas in case (B), the robot "thinks" we have directed him to listen. At this point, the robot is unable to respond because of the ambiguity.

Linguists have pondered this problem for several decades. The most successful extension of the model presented here consists of a semantic extension that converts one phrase-marker into another phrase-marker. Each phrase-marker conversion is called a *transformation*. For example, the robot might transform the phrase-marker from case (A) into the marker of case (B). Thus, the semantics alter, giving the robot an alternative "meaning" for the sentence.

A *transformational grammar* is a grammar that combines the syntactic rules of grammar with the transformational rules of semantics to yield a model of natural language.

Unfortunately, there are hundreds of rules used to approximate the semantics of written English. The time required to process all the known rules places a burden on even the most powerful computers. And, at present, it seems that the only computer capable of rapidly processing the transformational phrase-markers is between the ears of the reader.

In the final section of this chapter, we explain how to parse commands such as the one above: "Robot, come here." The techniques for recognizing limited English commands. It should be repeated that the bigger problem of meaning is not solved by such programs.

5.3 English Parsing Techniques

The techniques of the previous section deal mainly with the generation of sentences. What we will attempt to do in this section is describe how to reverse the process. We want to program a personal computer to parse a command in English, produce the phrase-marker, and ultimately act on the instructions of a human being.

Suppose that we want a robot to recognize the limited commands:

"Robot, turn to the left."
"Albert, turn right."
"You come here."
"Robot, go back."
"Albert, stop!"

What model provides rules for parsing such commands? What is the grammar for robot commands?

Grammar of Robot Commands

1. Command	= noun phrase + verb phrase
2. Noun phrase	= keyword
3. Verb phrase	= verb
	or, verb + adverbial phrase

4. Adverbial phrase	= adverb or, preposition + article + object
5. Keyword	= (robot, you, Albert)
6. Verb	= (go, come, turn, stop)
7. Adverb	= (right, back, here)
8. Preposition	= (to)
9. Article	= (the)
10. Object	= (left)

The grammar of robot commands is used to construct a phrase-marker for every command input to the computer. The process is called "bottom-up" parsing, because we start constructing the phrase-marker from its bottom to its top. For example, to construct the second phrase-marker of Fig. 5.6, we begin with the first word, "You."

noun phrase
|
keyword
|
you

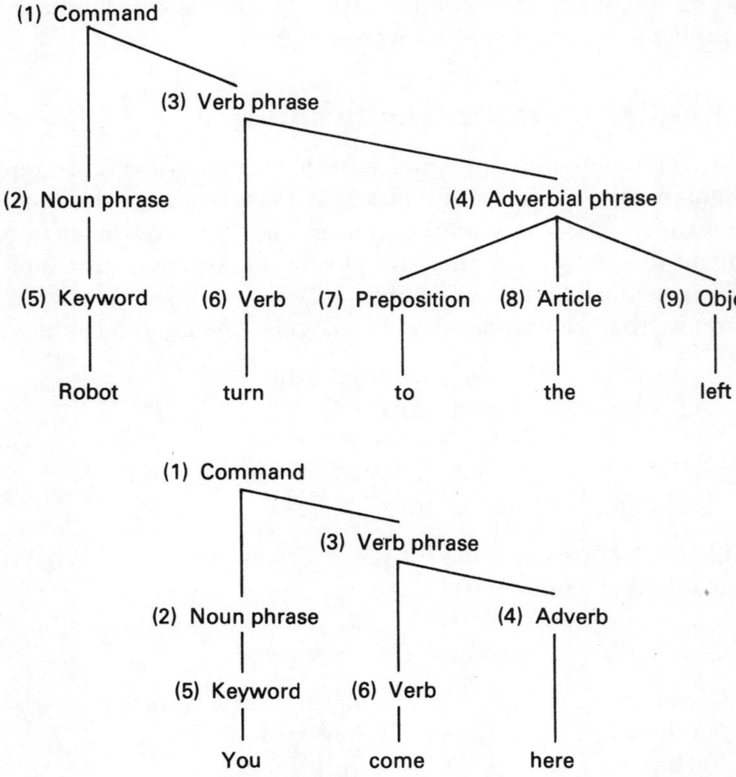

Fig. 5.6 Bottom-up parsing

The first part of the phrase-marker "tree" is the lower branch containing "you," and the parts of speech discernible at this stage of the parse. Since we cannot determine the root of the tree without additional input, we go on to the next word:

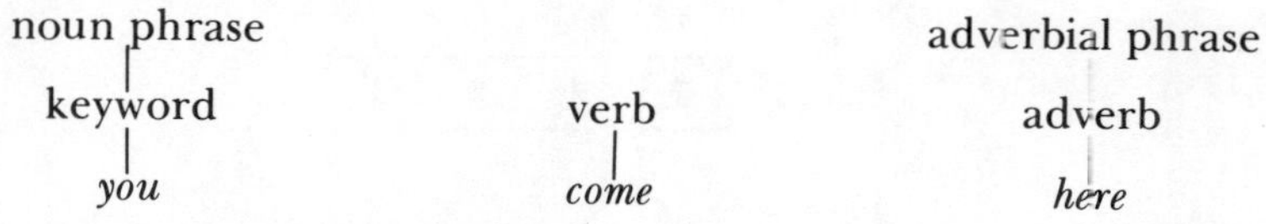

At this point in the bottom-up method, we realize that the branches can be "reduced" by combining them. Which ones can be combined? Looking at the right-hand side of the grammar rules, we find the matching rule:

$$\text{verb phrase} = \underbrace{\text{verb} + \text{adverbial phrase}}_{\text{right-hand-side matches}}$$

Once we recognize a right-hand side that allows a reduction, we can replace the branches with a root.

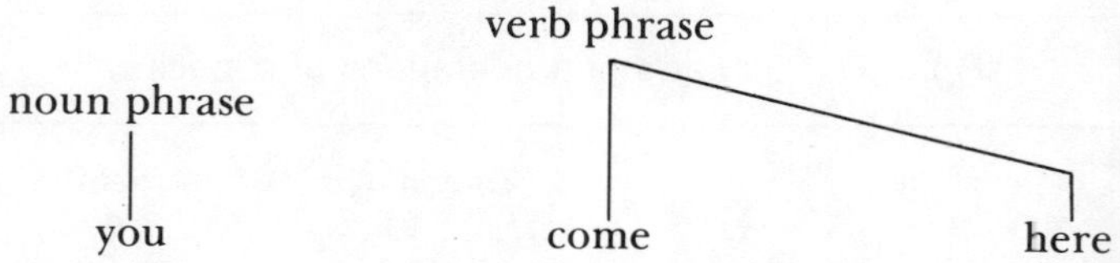

Again, we look for a matching right-hand side that will allow for the reduction of "noun phrase + verb phrase." The result of a search over the entire grammar produces a left-hand-side reduction to "command." The results of two bottom-up parses are shown in Fig. 5.6.

Every command sentence can be recognized by the bottom-up method. The only requirement necessary is that the grammar be unambiguous.

A computer program for bottom-up parsing combines the tree-growing part illustrated above with a search over the grammar. We can use a special device, called a *pushdown stack*, or simply a stack, to store the right-hand-sides while searching for a grammar rule. Once the grammar rule is found, the right-hand-side stored in the stack is replaced by the left-hand-side of the grammar rule.

A stack works as follows. Numbers are put *onto* the stack by *pushing* them and taken *off* the stack by *popping* them. The numbers come off the stack in reverse order. For example, Fig. 5.7 illustrates a pushdown stack at various stages of push or pop operation.

A pop operation removes the top element from a stack. A push operation places the new number on the top position of the stack. Hence, if we push the numbers 1, 2, 3, 4 onto a stack, they come off the stack as 4, 3, 2, 1.

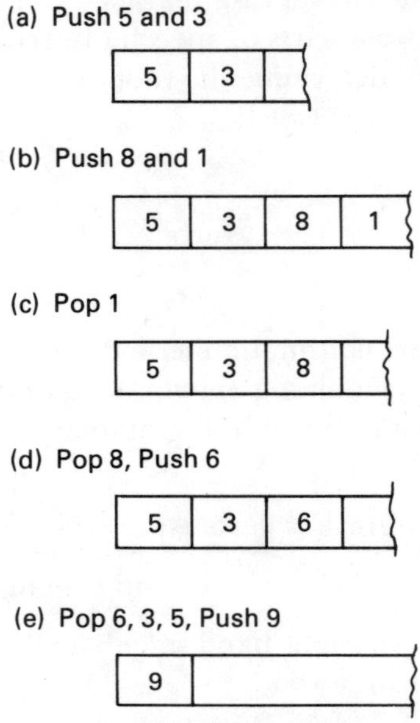

Fig. 5.7 Push and pop operations of a stack

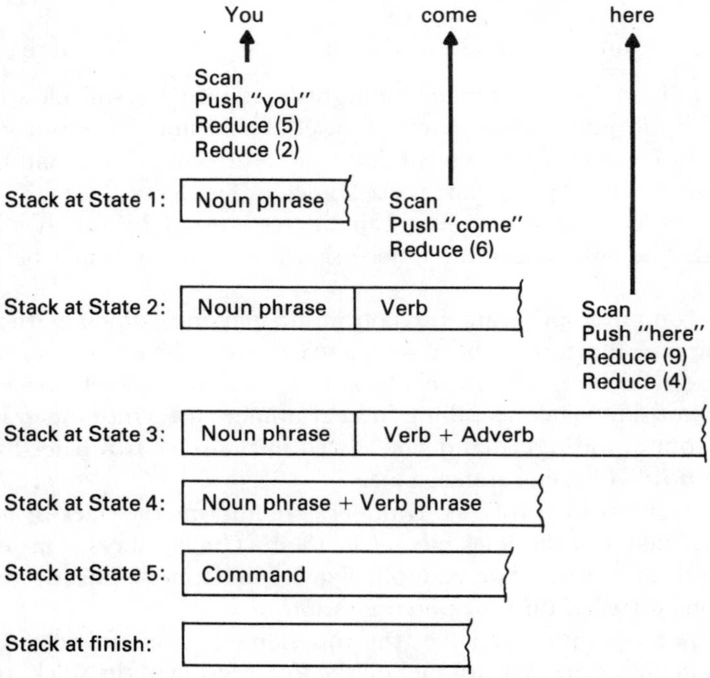

Fig. 5.8 Processing "You come here"

The grammar of robot commands is converted to numbers by encoding the words being used and the element of grammar they represent. Once we convert these elements to numbers, we simplify the push and pop operations and speed up the search for right-hand sides.

The encoded grammar is shown below (assume that every element is numbered from 101 to 110):

101 = 102 + 103
102 = 105
103 = 106 or 106 + 104
104 = 109 or 107 + 109 or 107 + 108 + 109
105 = robot, or you, or Albert
106 = go, or come, or turn, or stop
107 = right, or back, or here
108 = to, or in
109 = the
110 = left

Using the abbreviated grammar and the algorithm below, we can generate parse trees for robot commands.

Steps of the Algorithm

1. Read a word (listen)
   (a) Scan the input for a word
   (b) Compare it with words in the dictionary
2. Replace the word by its part of speech (push)
   (a) The dictionary entry will also determine the part of speech from the grammar.
   (b) Push the part of speech onto the stack
3. Repeat until no further reductions are possible (reduce)
   (a) Compare the top-of-stack elements with every right-hand side of every rule in the grammar
   (b) When a match occurs, replace the right-hand side with the rule's left-hand side. Discard the right-hand side (pop from stack) in the replacement process.
   (c) Carry out any (all) actions implied by the reduction in step (B). For example, if a verb, for example, "turn," is being reduced, then the robots should prepare to turn by a motor being actuated, etc.
4. These steps (1 to 3) are repeated until all words have been processed.

Let's apply the algorithm to the command, "You come here." The results are illustrated in Fig. 5.8, along with a stack showing the right-hand sides (in symbolic form rather than by using numbers).

A scan operation reads each word as input, one at a time. The word is immediately replaced by its part of speech. The part of speech is pushed onto the stack so that it (with preceding parts of speech) is matched against a right-hand side.

A reduce operation is performed each time the stack contains a right-hand side. The right-hand side is removed from the stack, and the left-hand side is pushed onto the stack.

Notice that the top-of-stack elements in Fig. 5.8 match the nodes in the parse tree of Fig. 5.6. We can tell when the root of the parse tree is reached whenever the stack contains the "command" symbol.

Each reduction of Fig. 5.8 is done by matching a rule to a right-hand side. The rule number is shown next to the reduction.

The techniques of this chapter provide a basis for further experimentation with personal computers. While the methods nearly solve the syntactic analysis problem, they leave the semantic problem unsolved. Semantics must be resolved during the reduction steps.

A personal computer equipped with sound-processing hardware is able to process audio input. Coupled with word-recognition hardware, and sound-processing software, a computer can function as a primitive robot. Personal computers with a voice response would truly be able to convince their masters that they are robots deserving of admiration.

Chapter Six

THE DEN (BUSINESS PROCESSING)

"John, you can't have the keys to the microcomputer until your homework is done! I just don't know where this latest generation of kids is going. . . . . no responsibility or ambition. All they want to do, it seems, is play with computers and drive around town."

Suburbia, 1980

John was always a quiet boy. He never got into trouble at school, and his friends were well-mannered. His father was baffled when he discovered that John was an information junkie.

"I don't know where we went wrong," John, Sr. lamented as he took aim on the fourth green. His putt was perfect, thus placing his golfing companion for the day—me—in a pressure situation. "I mean, Martha and I have always taught the kids to work hard and grow up to become lawyers or doctors. I don't want John, Jr., to have to work the way I did to make a success of himself."

"I'm not sure he has failed at anything. John," I said slowly, while measuring the cut of the grass. "I think, as a matter of fact, that John, Jr., has a great career ahead of him as a computer programmer." The ball rimmed the cup and rolled a few feet away.

"My God, I hope not!" John cried. "Programmers are an unruly, uncivilized bunch of freaks. You know that yourself."

"Come now, John, we aren't quite so different from bank executives. In fact, some of my best friends are programmers with a wife and kids like your own." I tried to be diplomatic about his attitude in spite of the fact that he was beating me by five strokes.

The truth is that John, Jr., has always been an information junkie —someone who collects unrelated, out-of-the way, usually useless, and sometimes esoteric facts. For example, many people know that the Empire State Building is nearly a quarter of a mile high (1248 feet), but John, Jr., also knows its weight (300,000 tons) and that it contains 63 elevators. He keeps up-to-date on important information like what happens inside a cat when it purrs, and why snow is white.

"What am I going to do with John?" he said, as we walked back to the clubhouse.

"Let me think it over, John, and I'll call you at the office, tomorrow. I think I can help."

The next day I called John and proposed a plan to help both father and son out of their stalemate. The plan was simple.

John, Jr., was to be allowed to spend as much time as he wanted with the household computer and eventually take up the profession of his choice. John, Sr., in exchange, was to receive a collection of programs to do useful work around his den.

John, Sr., accepted the plan, hoping that his son would tire of playing with computers. As it actually turned out, they both benefitted in the long run. John, Jr., continued with his studies as a computer scientist and returned to take over his father's position as president of the family corporation. One shouldn't be surprised to learn that the first change made by President John, Jr., was to computerize its accounting department.

6.1 A Checking System

The simplest task initiated by John, Jr., after his father accepted my plan was a check writer program. The program accepts check register data during the month. Then, upon demand, it prints all checks needed to pay the household bills.

Each record of the file containing check information consists of the following:

1. Date of check
2. Amount in dollars (in numbers)
3. Amount in dollars (in words)
4. Name of payee

The records of John's system are stored on a diskette. The diskette file appears as one long string of numbers and characters. Since the data are entered and the checks are printed in order, the file is organized sequentially. The basic pattern of file access is shown below:

```
3010    OPEN #1, "CHECKS"
3020    READ #1, D$
```

This sequence of code opens the sequential file named CHECKS and assigns it to logical unit #1. The READ command inputs the value of D$ from the first record of the file. In this case, D$ is the date of the check file (when it was created).

3070 READ #1, D$, A$, V$, W$

This command causes subsequent records to be input as required by the check writer. Finally, when the end-of-file mark on diskette is reached, the file is closed:

3060 IF TYP(1) = 0 THEN 3200

This statement tests the end-of-file condition, and if zero is matched, the file has been processed.

3220 CLOSE #1

The CLOSE command forces the last record to be processed and the logical file number to be released.

The program of Fig. 6.1 processes check information as follows: When the program is run, a menu appears on the screen. The menu allows a user to select one of four possible processing functions. The first function is used only once each time that checks are processed. The

```
LOAD CHECKWTR
READY
LIST
100 REM*********************************************
101 REM
102 REM      CHECK WRITER SYSTEM
103 REM
104 REM*********************************************
105 REM
110 DIM Y$(3),D$(15),A$(10),V$(60),W$(60)
120 REM
130 PRINT"CHECK WRITING SYSTEM AT YOUR SERVICE"
140 PRINT : PRINT : PRINT
150 PRINT"SELECT ONE OF THE FOLLOWING :"
160 PRINT
170 PRINT"            1. INITIALIZE THE SYSTEM."
171 PRINT"            2. ENTER BILLS AND THEIR AMOUNT"
172 PRINT"            3. PRINT CHECKS (OUTPUT)."
173 PRINT"            4. STOP."
174 PRINT
175 INPUT"ENTER CHOICE :",N
180 REM
181 REM---------CALL APPROPRIATE ROUTINE-------------
182 REM
190 ON N GOTO 210,220,230,410
200 GOTO 150
```

Fig. 6.1 Check writer program

```
201 REM
210 GOSUB 1000 : GOTO 150
220 GOSUB 2000 : GOTO 150
230 GOSUB 3000 : GOTO 150
400 REM
410 END
800 REM*********************************************************
801 REM
802 REM        CONVERT A$ TO A1 (A NUMBER)
803 REM
804 REM*********************************************************
805 REM
806 LET L=LEN(A$)
810 FOR I=1 TO L
812 IF I>LEN(A$) THEN 814 ELSE 820
814 EXIT 910
820 IF A$(I,I)="$" THEN 860 ELSE 830
830 IF A$(I,I)="," THEN 860 ELSE 900
850 GOTO 900
860 REM
870 REM------------SQUEEZE OUT NON DIGITS--------------------
880 REM
890 LET A$(I)=A$(I+1)
900 NEXT I
910 LET A1=INT(100*VAL(A$))/100
920 RETURN
1000 REM*****************************************************
1001 REM
1002 REM      INITIALIZE THE FILE
1003 REM
1004 REM*****************************************************
1005 REM
1010 OPEN #1,"CHECKS"
1020 INPUT"DATE OF FILE CREATION :",D$
1030 WRITE #1,D$,"CHECKWRITER"
1040 CLOSE #1
1050 REM
1060 PRINT"CHECKWRITER FILE INITIALIZED ON ",D$
1070 PRINT : PRINT : PRINT : PRINT : PRINT
1080 RETURN
2000 REM*****************************************************
2001 REM
2002 REM     ENTER BILL INFORMATION
2003 REM
2004 REM*****************************************************
2005 REM
2010 OPEN #1,"CHECKS"
2020 READ #1,D$
2030 PRINT"BEGIN ENTERING INFORMATION FOR DATE :",D$
2035 PRINT : PRINT : PRINT
2050 REM
2051 REM-----------LOOP ON INPUT---------------------------
2052 REM
2060 INPUT"DATE OF CHECK :",D$
2070 IF D$="" THEN 2200 : REM RETURN >>>>>>>>>>>>>>>>>>>>>>>>:
2080 INPUT"AMOUNT IN $,$$$.CC : ",A$
2090 INPUT"AMOUNT IN ENGLISH : ",V$
```

Fig. 6.1 Check writer program (cont'd)

```
2100 INPUT"PAY TO THE ORDER OF : ",W$
2110 PRINT : INPUT" OK ? ",Y$
2120 REM
2130 IF Y$="YES" THEN 2150 ELSE 2060
2135 REM
2136 REM-----------WRITE RECORD TO FILE--------------------
2137 REM
2150 WRITE #1,D$,A$,V$,W$
2155 PRINT : PRINT : PRINT : PRINT : PRINT : PRINT : PRINT
2160 GOTO 2060
2170 REM-----------END OF INPUT LOOP-----------------------
2171 REM
2200 CLOSE #1
2210 RETURN
3000 REM***************************************************
3001 REM
3002 REM             PRINT CHECKS
3003 REM
3004 REM***************************************************
3005 REM
3010 OPEN #1,"CHECKS"
3020 READ #1,D$
3030 REM
3035 PRINT"CHECK WRITER FOR DATE : ",D$
3040 PRINT : PRINT : PRINT : PRINT
3050 LET S=0 : REM S IS THE TOTAL AMOUNT PAID OUT.
3055 REM
3056 REM-----------LOOP ON OUTPUT--------------------------
3057 REM
3060 IF TYP(1)=0 THEN 3200 : REM RETURN >>>>>>>>>>>>>>>>>
3070 READ #1,D$,A$,V$,W$
3080 REM
3090 PRINT TAB(30),D$
3100 PRINT TAB(35),A$
3110 PRINT"PAY TO : ",W$
3120 PRINT"==================================================="
3130 PRINT
3140 PRINT"PAY ",V$," DOLLARS"
3145 PRINT"..................................................."
3150 PRINT : PRINT : PRINT
3160 PRINT TAB(25),"------------------------"
3170 PRINT TAB(30),"SIGNATURE"
3175 PRINT : PRINT : PRINT : PRINT : PRINT
3180 REM
3181 REM-----------TOTAL VALUE-----------------------------
3182 REM
3190 GOSUB 800
3191 LET S=S+A1
3195 GOTO 3060
3199 REM
3200 REM-----------TERMINATE-------------------------------
3201 REM
3210 PRINT"  TOTAL PAID OUT = ",%C$,S
3220 CLOSE #1
3230 RETURN
3240 REM
READY
```

Fig. 6.1 Check writer program (cont'd)

INITIALIZE function writes a date out to the file as the first record of the file. If the CHECKS file has not been created earlier, this step will notify the user of an error condition.

The ENTER BILLS function is executed so as to enter data pertinent to each check. The data are entered by prompting input, as shown in lines 2060–2110.

The PRINT CHECKS function reads the sequential file and prints one check for each record of the file. The total amount paid is computed as S, and output is computed as the last printed number.

Note in line 3190 a call to a subprogram at location 800. The dollars and cents amount of each check is entered as a string variable, A$. The subprogram at location 800 converts the digits stored in A$ to a number, A1. Study lines 806–850 to see how this conversion is accomplished. Lines 860–890 squeeze out any nondigit character by moving the digits together. Finally, line 910 produces a dollars-and-cents value in A1 by placing the decimal point two digits to the left of the least significant digit in A1.

When this program is run on a computer with a printer, it is capable of printing values and names on check forms. The forms are signed (and verified, of course) by John, Sr., and sent to the creditor. This relieves John and Martha of the painful chore of writing checks.

John, Jr., was pleased enough with the check writer program to tackle his next application with equal vigor.

6.2 A Household Budget System

The idea behind a budget system is to control the amount of money spent over a period of time. Ideally, a budget is worked out in advance and used to review expenditures and aid in income tax reporting at the end of the year as well as to govern day-by-day spending.

John's budget system works from a very simple chart-of-accounts ledger. Each entry consists of a DATE of expenditure, TITLE of budgeted item, allocated budget, amount expended, year-to-date total expended, and percent of total budget actually spent. These values are stored in the program of Fig. 6.2 as the following variables:

D$	Date
T$	Title
M	Budget amount
E	Actual amount
Y	Year-to-date spent
P	Percent spent

The program of Fig. 6.2 is straightforward except for the method of file access, which was dictated by the dialect of BASIC employed by John. Although not actually needed, I/O to each record is accomplished by

```
LOAD BUDGET
READY
LIST
100 REM ************************************************************
101 REM
102 REM      HOUSEHOLD BUDGET SYSTEM
103 REM
104 REM ************************************************************
105 REM
110 DIM D$(12),T$(20),M$(10),N$(10)
111 REM
112 INPUT"ENTER MONTH :",M$
115 REM
120 PRINT"SELECT ONE OF THE FOLLOWING"
125 PRINT : PRINT : PRINT : PRINT
130 PRINT"            1. INPUT ACCOUNTS (INITIALIZE)."
131 PRINT"            2. INPUT MONTHLY EXPENSES."
132 PRINT"            3. PRINT BUDGET SHEET."
133 PRINT"            4. STOP."
140 PRINT : PRINT : PRINT : PRINT : PRINT : PRINT
150 INPUT"ENTER CHOICE :",J
155 REM
156 REM--------------SELECT A ROUTINE ---------------------
157 REM
160 ON J GOTO 180,190,200,210,120
170 REM
180        GOSUB 1000 : PRINT"INITIALIZED CHART" : GOTO 120
190        GOSUB 2000 : PRINT"END MONTHLY INPUT" : GOTO 120
200        GOSUB 3000 : PRINT"PRINTING FINISHED" : GOTO 120
210 REM
220 PRINT"ENTER 'RUN' TO START PROGRAM, AGAIN" : STOP
1000 REM *******************************************************
1001 REM
1002 REM      INPUT ACCOUNTS (INITIALIZE)
1003 REM
1004 REM *******************************************************
1005 REM
1010 INPUT"ENTER MAXIMUM NUMBER OF ACCOUNTS :",N
1020 OPEN #1,M$
1030 WRITE #1 %0,M$,N
1040 LET D$="------------" : E=0 : Y=0 : P=0
1045 REM
1046 REM -------INITIALIZATION OF HEADER INFO, DONE---------
1047 REM
1050 FOR I=1 TO N
1060    INPUT"ENTER A 20 CHAR. TITLE :",T$
1070    IF T$="" THEN 1080 ELSE 1090
1080    EXIT 1200
1088    REM >>>>>>>>>>>>>>>>>>>>>>>>>>>>>>>>>>>>>>>>>>>>>>>>>
1090    INPUT"ENTER BUDGETED AMOUNT $.C :",M
1100    WRITE #1 %56*I+17,D$,T$,M,E,Y,P
1150 NEXT I
1200 CLOSE #1
1250 RETURN
2000 REM *******************************************************
2001 REM
2002 REM      INPUT MONTHLY EXPENSES
```

Fig. 6.2 Household budget program

```
2003 REM
2004 REM *****************************************************
2005 REM
2010 OPEN #1,M$
2020 READ #1 %0,N$,N
2030 IF M$=N$ THEN 2050 ELSE 2200
2040 REM
2041 REM -----UPDATE CHART OF ACCOUNTS---------------------
2042 REM
2050 FOR I=1 TO N
2060     READ #1 %56*I+17,D$,T$,M,E,Y,P
2070     PRINT "    ",T$," <<<<<ENTER>>>>>"
2080     REM
2090     INPUT"ENTER DATE OF BILL :",D$
2100     INPUT"ENTER AMOUNT OF BILL :",E
2105     REM
2110     IF M=0 THEN P=0 ELSE P=100*(E/M)
2115     REM
2120     LET Y1=Y+E
2130     PRINT"DATE=",D$," ' ",T$,"BUDGET=",M," EXPENDED=",
2131     PRINT E," YTD=",Y1," %=",P
2140     INPUT"IS THIS CORRECT ? (Y/N) :",Y$
2150     IF Y$="N" THEN 2090
2160     REM
2165     LET Y=Y1
2170     WRITE #1 %56*I+17,D$,T$,M,E,Y,P
2190 NEXT I
2200 CLOSE #1
2250 RETURN
3000 REM *********************************************************
3001 REM
3002 REM    PRINT REPORT OF BUDGET
3003 REM
3004 REM *********************************************************
3005 REM
3010 OPEN #1,M$
3020 READ #1 %0,N$,N
3030 IF M$=N$ THEN 3050 ELSE 3200
3040 LET S1=0 : S2=0 : S3=0 :S4=0 : REM INITIAL SUMS
3050 REM
3055 PRINT"DATE",TAB(13),"TITLE",TAB(36),"BUDGET EXPENDED",
3056 PRINT " YEAR-TO-DATE PERCENT"
3057 PRINT"--------------------------------------------------",
3058 PRINT"------------------"
3060 FOR I=1 TO N
3070     READ #1 %56*I+17,D$,T$,M,E,Y,P
3075     PRINT D$," ' ",T$,TAB(36),%$C5F2,M,
3076     PRINT %$C6F2,E,TAB(55),%$C7F2,Y,%8F1,P,"%"
3090     LET S1=S1+M : S2=S2+E : S3=S3+Y : S4=S4+P
3100 NEXT I
3150 PRINT " TOTALS FOR EACH COLUMN :"
3160 PRINT"--------------------------------------------------"
3170 PRINT TAB(36),%$C5F2,S1,%$C6F2,S2,
3171 PRINT TAB(55),%$C7F2,S3,%8F1,S4,"%"
3180 REM
3200 CLOSE #1
3250 RETURN
READY
```

Fig. 6.2 Household budget program (cont'd)

means of random, or direct, access. The name of the budget file is stored as record zero. (See lines 1030, 2020, 3020.) Each subsequent access to the random file is made by computing the beginning location of each record in the file stored as a single string:

```
1100      WRITE #1, %56*I + 17, D$, T$, M, E, Y, P
```

The percent sign indicates (via the BASIC interpreter) that random access is being used. The location of record I is computed knowing that each record takes 56 characters of disk space. The first record (location zero) is 17 characters long. Thus, to access record 3, we compute its location in the string as 56(3) + 17, or 185.

The percent sign is used in another unusual way in the program of Fig. 6.2. In line 3076, it controls output formatting. The dollar sign indicates that the following number is a dollars-and-cents number to be preceded by a $ sign. The C indicates that a comma should be inserted where needed to help readability. The 6F2 indicates that a six-digit number, with two digits to the right of the decimal point, is to be printed.

The ledgers produced by John's budgeting program delighted his father. For once, the son really pleased the old man, and the latter decided that there might be a place for information junkies, after all.

6.3 The Income Tax System

John had little trouble programming the family microcomputer to print income tax returns. His program handles initialization of a file, data entry (building the file), and processing and printing in the same manner as the other programs.

The biggest difficulties in an income tax program are twofold:

1. The amounts needed must be computed in the proper order. If the calculations are not done exactly as they should be, then printing (on the form) cannot take place without backing up the printer.
2. The tax return form must be lined up precisely so that all printing takes place in the space provided for it.

After John perfected his income tax system, he made an interesting discovery. The IRS accepts returns on machine readable tape or diskette! The IRS sent John a description of the diskette format used by the IRS computer. John reprogrammed his microcomputer to conform with the IRS format and did away with paper altogether!

Now, John, Jr. and Sr., enjoy the evening of April 14th by the fire. They drink hot rum and listen contentedly while the family household computer clicks in the den.

From these humble beginnings, John went on to design and implement dozens of useful financial programs. The resultant "package" of programs performed cash flow analysis, stock market analysis, and electronic funds transfer over the telephone.

Chapter Seven

THE BATHROOM (GRAPHICS)

"I did my best work on the walls of the boys' room at Elementary School #PS–3015. In those days we spent as much time in the stalls as we could, to avoid Miss Cratchett. If I ever return to that school, my first impulse will be to look in the restrooms to see if my contribution lived on after me."

Confession of a graffitoist

Charlie's mother had a right to be unhappy with him. In the fifth grade, his report cards were at best marginal. By the time he finished the sixth grade, he had established a reputation as "King of the Latrine." Needless to say, his throne was on the other side of the door marked "Boys."

The eighth grade posed a challenge for both Charlie and his parents. His mother pushed him into the analyst's chair of the school counselor, into the study of their minister's parish house, and, finally, into the clinic of two specialists dealing in hyperactive children. If at all possible, she was determined that Charlie was going to get straightened out before the first day of class.

Charlie simply loved to draw pictures on walls. He considered himself an artist, a special kind of artist. Charlie's mother failed to understand how tempting the clean, white school walls were to a true artist. Consequently, Charlie's well-paved way into the eighth grade turned out to be a fiasco.

On the second day of class, Charlie was promptly sent home. Everything had been tried, and nothing had worked. Charlie's mother called me in desperation.

"I must have gone wrong somewhere," she wept over the 'phone. "Charlie has always been a sweet, well-behaved child in every other respect, but his graffiti is causing social problems."

"I see," was my cautious reply. "Have you thought of electric shock or sending him to a private school in Iceland?"

Charlie's mother insisted that I see the two of them on Friday, so we agreed on a time. After hanging up the telephone, I thought for a long time about Charlie's problem. Clearly, the solution was a personal computer system, but exactly how could it be used in this peculiar case?

7.1 Introduction to Pictures

Charlie, I am happy to report, was cured after two visits to my laboratory. His mother and I agreed that a personal computer with graphics capability would provide him with a proper outlet for his talents. Events proved that we were right. After several weeks, Charlie gave up on restroom walls and devoted all of his spare time to his personal computer.

Incidentally, Charlie grew up and became a manager of a drug store. He never lost interest in computer graphics, however, and still uses his system at home. Many of the techniques discussed in this chapter were developed by Charlie.

Personal computers that can draw may be purchased in one of two forms:

Refresh Graphics

A refresh tube is quite similar to a TV tube (identical in many cases). The picture is "painted" 30 or 40 times a second so that a human eye cannot see a flicker on the screen.

Typically, a refresh screen requires a memory to store the displayed data. The memory is read 30 to 40 times per second in order to paint the picture. If the picture is changed, the newly modified data stored in the memory provided by the display unit is painted on the screen. For example, to move a point across the face of a TV screen, we must store a character representing the point in one cell of the memory for a second, then erase it and store it in another cell for a second, and so forth. Unfortunately, one of the problems with refresh graphics in the high cost of backing memory needed to store the picture.

Refresh graphics is useful for interaction with the computer. A user can change parts of the picture and see the change take place immediately.

Suppose that we want to plot points on a grid of 100 by 100 points. The memory needed to store these points exceeds 10,000 characters. If we attempt to reduce the grid to 50 by 50, we also reduce the *resolution* of the picture. Resolution is the measure of its granularity.

One solution to the memory problem is to store the picture directly on the face of the scope. Personal computers that include storage screen scopes are called *display graphics*, or *storage-type* computers.

Storage Graphics

A storage tube differs from a TV tube in that it can store a picture for many weeks without being refreshed. The screen may be totally erased and a picture redrawn, but the amount of interaction possible between a user and the picture is reduced.

Suppose that we want to display a pie chart on a storage screen. The system is directed to draw a circle along with several radii that divide the circle into "pie" sections. The storage screen is able to store the pie chart for a long time after it is drawn.

If the pie chart is to be modified, the storage scope must be erased and the pie chart redrawn. In a refresh system, the pie chart can be immediately altered through the data stored in the refresh backing memory.

Many BASIC language personal computers provide programmers with the tools to draw pictures in the form of extended BASIC commands. In the examples developed in this chapter, we will assume extensions to BASIC for drawing, moving, and scaling picture information.

The WINDOW command,

WINDOW   low X, high X, low Y, high Y

establishes a scale for the pictures drawn on the screen. The values of low X, high X, low Y, high Y are expressed in the user's units. For example, if we want to draw a picture 10 ft wide, and 20 ft high, we might use the following command:

WINDOW   0, 10, 0, 20

Alternatively, if we want to plot a curve running from (–100) to (+100) in the X-direction, and (–10) to (+10) in the Y-direction, we use the following WINDOW command:

WINDOW   –100, 100, –10, 10

Such a personal computer uses WINDOW to adjust the picture to fit within the scale indicated by WINDOW.

The AXIS command,

AXIS   X-size, Y-size

draws an X, Y axis in the space provided by a WINDOW. The X-size parameter informs the system to place a tick mark on the X-axis at intervals separated by X-size user units. The Y-size parameter specifies that the Y-axis be marked for Y-size units along the axis.

The command,

AXIS 5, 10

causes an X, Y axis to be drawn with tick marks at 5, 10, 15, 20, 25, . . . along the X-axis, and tick marks at 10, 20, 30, 40, . . . along the Y-axis.

We use the AXIS command to draw the axis for an X, Y coordinate system. The coordinates are used to plot a curve that is given by a mathematical equation.

The VIEWPORT command,

VIEWPORT start X, stop X, start Y, stop Y

locates a physical section of the screen for placing the picture. In the system used for illustrations, the screen is divided into 130 horizontal points and 100 vertical points. Thus, the physical screen is a grid of 130 by 100 points.

The command,

VIEWPORT 30, 130, 0, 100

results in the picture's appearing on the screen 30 units to the right of the lower left-hand corner. The right-hand border is at location 130 (as far right as the picture can go), and the bottom of the picture is at the bottom of the screen.

The command,

VIEWPORT 64, 65, 49, 51

causes the picture to be forced into a small square one unit by two units high, centered in the middle of the screen.

The command,

MOVE X, Y

causes the "paint brush" to be picked up and moved to location X, Y. No lines are drawn. The paint brush is called a *cursor.* We move the cursor from where it currently points to a new location X, Y (relative to the lower right-hand corner of the WINDOW inside the VIEWPORT).

The DRAW command,

DRAW X, Y

performs exactly the same way as the MOVE command except that it draws a straight line as it moves to position X, Y. It is the fundamental command for drawing lines on the screen.

The PAGE command,

PAGE

erases everything from a storage screen, whereas the HOME command,

HOME

causes the cursor to position itself at the upper, left-hand corner of the screen. It is used to restore the cursor before printing messages on the display screen.

Other graphics commands may be included in BASIC. For example, ROTATE is useful for rotating a picture; SET DEGREES is used to change from radian to degrees when calculating angles. In most cases, however, the seven commands described above are sufficient for computer graphics.

7.2 The New Geometry

In order to draw pictures on a screen, all we need to do is write a sequence of DRAW commands and let the computer do the rest. We initialize the screen by issuing WINDOW and VIEWPORT commands, and, in some cases, include an AXIS command:

```
100    VIEWPORT    0, 130, 0, 100
110    WINDOW      0, 10, 0, 10
120    MOVE        0, 0
130    DRAW        0, 10
140    DRAW        10, 10
150    DRAW        10, 0
160    DRAW        0, 0
```

This segment of BASIC code draws a rectangle on the screen. The MOVE 0, 0 command positions the cursor at the lower, left-hand corner of the WINDOW. Lines 130 through 160 trace out the rectangle one side at a time.

We can draw any polygon in the fashion shown above. In order to draw curvilinear figures, we must approximate curves with many short straight-line segments. Thus a circle, for example, is approximated by a polygon with hundreds of straight sides. Figure 7.1 illustrates improved approximations to a circle.

In order to draw a variety of shapes, we need a new approach to geometry. The new approach we employ requires some mathematics called trigonometry. Consider the following trigonometric relations.

The sine (SIN) of an angle is a mathematical function that ranges from minus one to plus one in magnitude. It oscillates between (– 1) and (+1) as the angle goes from zero to 360 degrees. The cosine (COS) of an angle oscillates in the same fashion as the SIN except that it is 90 degrees out-of-step with the SIN function. Hence,

$$\text{SIN}(A) = -\text{COS}(A + 90)$$

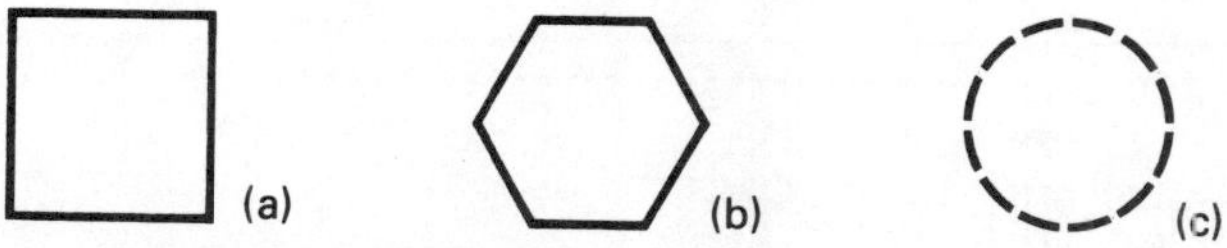

Fig. 7.1 Approximations to a circle

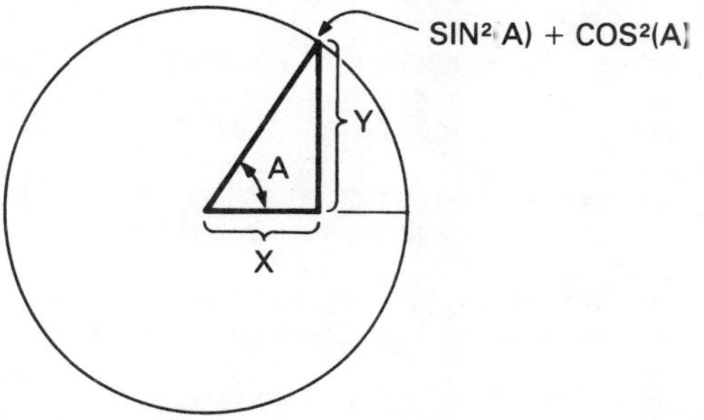

Fig. 7.2 Geometric functions of SIN and COS

Our new approach to geometry is based on the fact that a circle is completely defined by the sum of SIN^2 and COS^2:

$$1 = SIN^2(A) + COS^2(A)$$

Figure 7.2 illustrates the relationship between a circle with radius equal to 1 and the formula above. To compute the length of X and Y, we note that:

$$X = (\text{radius})\ COS(A)$$
$$Y = (\text{radius})\ SIN(A)$$

Hence, we have enough information to develop DRAW commands for a circle with radius R.

```
500     FOR A = 0 to 360 STEP 5
510     DRAW R*COS(A), R*SIN(A)
520     NEXT A
```

This segment of code draws straight-line segments at 5 degree intervals around the circumference of a circle with radius R. In short, the DRAW command sweeps out 360 degrees as the FOR loop increments A. The straight lines leave a trail approximating a circle's circumference. We will generalize this code to include a variety of figures.

Suppose that we want to draw a figure that is a function of the angle, A. We can define the function in a "define function" subprogram in BASIC. An EXP function, for example, produces a spiral:

```
160     DEF FNR(A) = -EXP(P*A)
```

```
100 REM ***********************************
110 REM
120 REM          COMPUTER GEOMETRY
130 REM
140 REM ***********************************
150 REM
160 PRINT "INPUT SCALE FACTOR M=";
170 INPUT M
180 PRINT "INPUT NUMBER OF POINTS N=";
190 INPUT N
200 PRINT "INPUT NUMBER OF TURNS S=";
210 INPUT S
220 REM **********DEFINE FUNCTION **************
230 PRINT "INPUT FUNCTION PARAMETER P=";
240 INPUT P
250 DEF FNR(A)=P*SIN(A)*COS(A)^2
260 REM ***********SET-UP GRAPHICS********
270 REM
280 PRINT "INPUT SIZE OF WINDOW X1,Y1=";
290 INPUT X1,Y1
300 WINDOW -X1,X1,-Y1,Y1
310 VIEWPORT 30,130,0,100
320 PAGE
330 AXIS 1,1
340 MOVE -X1,Y1
350 DRAW X1,Y1
360 DRAW X1,-Y1
370 DRAW -X1,-Y1
380 DRAW -X1,Y1
390 MOVE 0,0
400 REM***********BEGIN DRAWING *********
410 SET DEGREES
420 FOR I=1 TO N
430 LET T=360*S*I/N
440 DRAW M*FNR(T)*COS(T),M*FNR(T)*SIN(T)
450 NEXT I
460 HOME
470 PRINT USING 510:M
480 PRINT USING 520:N
490 PRINT USING 530:S
500 PRINT USING 540:X1,Y1
510 IMAGE "M=",3D.3D
520 IMAGE "N=",3D.3D
530 IMAGE "S=",3D.3D
540 IMAGE "X1,Y1=",3D," ",3D
550 END
```

Fig. 7.3 Generalized routine for computer geometry

The BASIC program of Figure 7.3 illustrates such a generalized program for plotting a function that varies with the angle of sweep, A. The output from this program is shown in Fig. 7.4.

Once we have the general program of Fig. 7.3, we can modify line 160 to change the sweeping function. For example, Figs. 7.5 and 7.6 illustrate what happens when the function is changed to SIN(12*A) and SIN(A*A), respectively.

M = 1.000
N = 200.000
S = 5.000
P = 0.001
X1, Y1 = 4 4

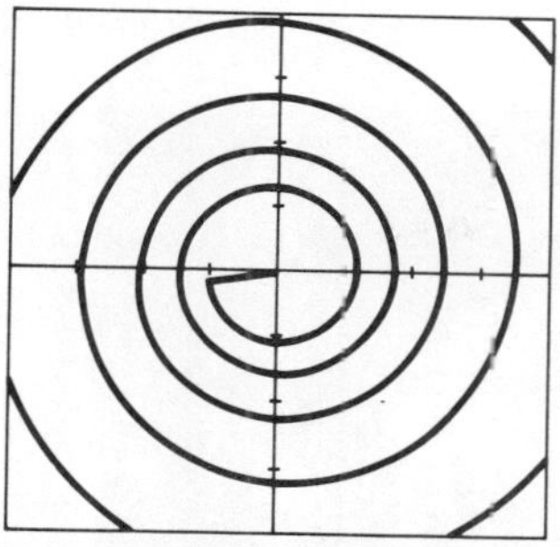

Fig. 7.4 Output for Fig. 7.3: DFN = – EXP(P*A)

Geometric figures can be developed into art forms with a small amount of experimentation. This kind of mathematics can be fun (see Figs. 7.7 and 7.8).

Figures 7.9 through 7.17 illustrate other modifications to the basic computer geometry program. In many of the "interesting" pictures, a random number is used to vary the figure in unexpected ways.

Fig. 7.5 12-petal flower: SIN(12A)

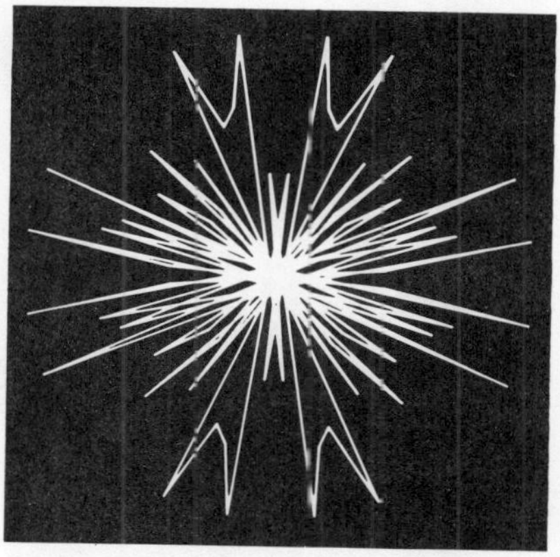

Fig. 7.6 "Omnibus": SIN(A^2)

Fig. 7.7 "Butterfly": SIN(5A)COS (3A)

Fig. 7.8 SIN(6A)COS(5A)

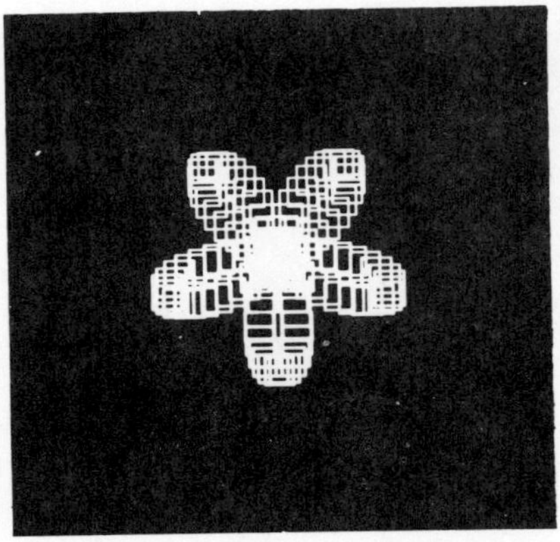

Fig. 7.9 Boxes on 5-petal flower

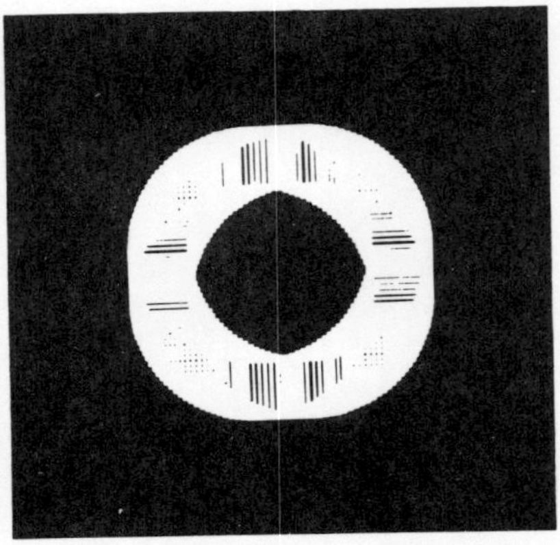

Fig. 7.10 Boxes on circle

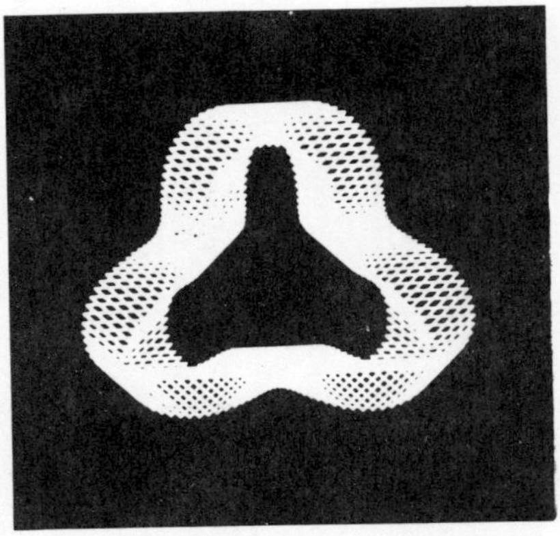

Fig. 7.11 Triangle: 1 + [SIN(3A)/3]

Fig. 7.12 Fan: $\rho_1 \cos \Theta$, $\rho_1 \sin \Theta$; $\rho_2 \cos \Theta$, $\rho_2 \sin \Theta$

Fig. 7.13 [(1 + SIN[8A])/8]/1.25

Fig. 7.14 [(1 + RND[1])/5]/1.5

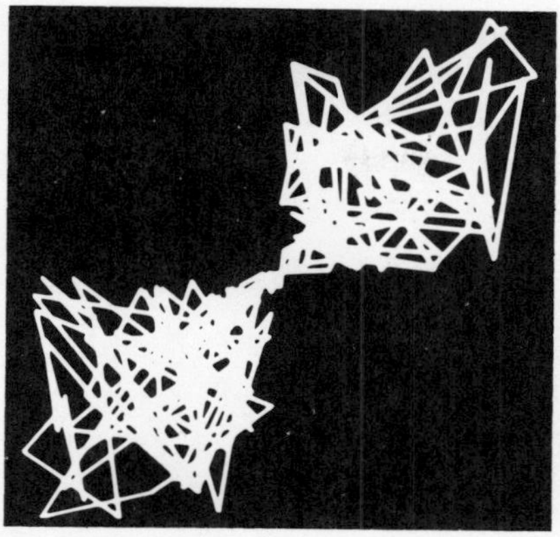

Fig. 7.15 For I = 0 to 360 Step 3, M*SIN(I)*RND(1), SIN(I)RND(1)*M

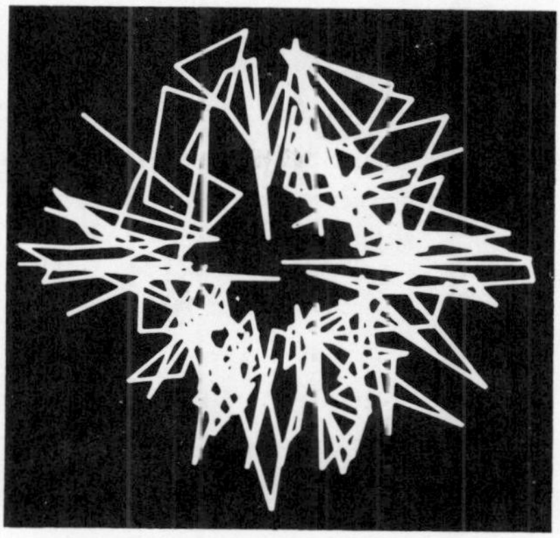

Fig. 7.16 Random-radius circle

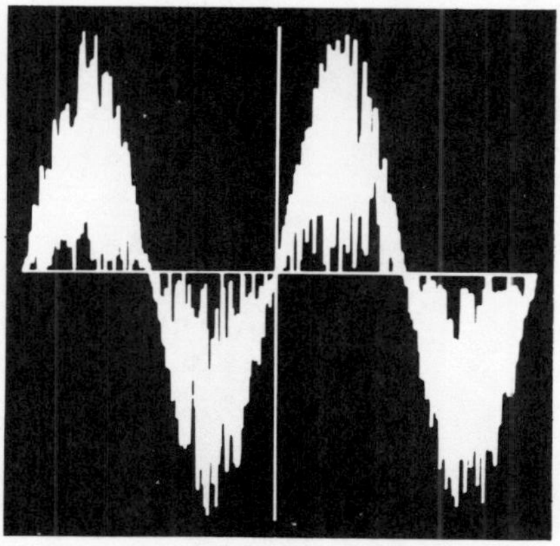

Fig. 7.17 "RANDOM SINE": x = x (−M,M); y = RND(1)*SIN(Θ)

7.3 Drawing for Fun

The geometric figures of the previous section may require more mathematical ability than you will need in order to enjoy graphics. Therefore, in this section we will develop a program that illustrates how to program a graphical game.

Suppose that we draw a large square on the screen and randomly position a target within the square. The object of the game is to select an angle and distance for shooting at the target. If the angle is too large or too small, the target will be missed. If the distance is estimated incorrectly, the torpedo will fall short or pass by the target.

The game is seemingly simple, but it becomes more challenging as the power of the explosion decreases. Suppose we use a pea-powered torpedo. The target is demolished only if a direct hit occurs. On the other hand, suppose we shoot at the target with an atomic torpedo. The atomic explosion will wipe out the target by merely coming close to it.

The game is scored by a formula that considers how many shots were used (how many torpedoes) and the size of the explosion:

$$\text{Score} = 10(N - I + 1)/(C*N)$$

where

N = Number of torpedoes requested
I = Actual number of torpedoes used
C = Size of charge (1 = spit, 10 = atomic)

The highest score is obtained by hitting the target on the first trial with a spit torpedo. When N = 1, I = 1, and C = 1, you will make a perfect score of 10.

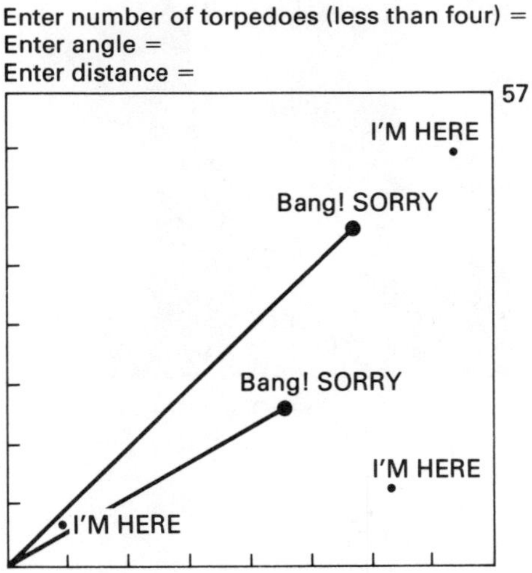

Fig. 7.18 Torpedo game output

The program for producing the output of Fig. 7.18 is shown in Fig. 7.19. Note the circle generator in lines 1110 to 1190. The circle is centered at X1, Y1, and its radius is R.

Another feature of the program of Fig. 7.19 is the segment of code that tests the hit-or-no-hit condition. Lines 790 to 840 illustrate how to use the ABS (absolute value) function to test the distance between the torpedo explosion and the target.

We can develop a variety of programs for graphical personal computers. The examples shown here helped to keep Charlie out of trouble, and they may help you get started in graphics.

```
100 REM*********************************************
110 REM
120 REM       TORPEDOES AWAY !!!!
130 REM
140 REM*********************************************
150 REM
160 REM----------INITIALIZE----------------------
170 REM
180 SET DEGREES
190 IMAGE 4D
200 IMAGE "YOUR SCORE IS=",2D.2D,"(MAX=10)"
210 DIM Y$(3)
220 HOME
230 REM
240 REM---------GET INPUT VALUES----------------------
250 REM
260 PRINT "man your battle stations !!"
270 PRINT "size of ocean (10<m<200)=";
280 INPUT M
290 IF M>200 THEN 270
300 PRINT "size of charge (1=spit,...10=atomic bomb)=";
310 INPUT C
320 IF C>10 THEN 300
330 PAGE
340 REM
350 REM----------SET UP GRAPHICS----------------------
360 REM
370 VIEWPORT 30,120,8,98
380 WINDOW 0,M,0,M
390 AXIS 5,5
400 MOVE 0,M
410 DRAW M,M
420 PRINT USING 190:M*SQR(2)
430 MOVE M,M
440 DRAW M,0
450 HOME
460 PRINT "enter no. of torpedoes (less than 4)=";
470 INPUT N
480 IF N>4 THEN 460
490 REM
500 REM-------------LOOP N TIMES FOR SHOTS--------------
510 REM
520 FOR I=1 TO N
530 LET X=M*RND(1)
540 LET Y=M*RND(1)
550 MOVE X,Y
560 PRINT ".I'M HERE!"
570 HOME
580 PRINT
590 PRINT "enter angle=";
600 INPUT A
610 PRINT "enter distance=";
620 INPUT D
630 MOVE 0,0
640 LET X1=D*COS(A)
650 LET Y1=D*SIN(A)
```

Fig. 7.19 Torpedo game program

```
660 DRAW X1,Y1
670 PRINT "bang!";
680 LET R=M*(C/100)
690 REM
700 REM----------DRAW CIRCLE--------------------------
710 REM
720 GOSUB 1110
730 IF ABS(X1-X)<=R THEN 750
740 GO TO 760
750 IF ABS(Y1-Y)<=R THEN 900
760 PRINT "too bad !"
770 NEXT I
780 REM
790 REM----------------END OF LOOP--------------------
800 REM
810 HOME
820 PRINT
830 PRINT
840 PRINT
850 PRINT "out of ammo---retreat!!"
860 GO TO 930
870 REM
880 REM----------------A HIT ! -------------------------
890 REM
900 PRINT "ouch !!"
910 LET S=10*(N-I+1)/(C*N)
920 PRINT USING 200:S
930 PRINT
940 PRINT "try again ?"
950 PRINT
960 PRINT "enter (yes or no)";
970 INPUT Y$
980 PAGE
990 IF Y$="yes" THEN 220
1000 REM
1010 REM-----------COMPUTE SCORE------------------------
1020 REM
1030 LET S=10*(N-I+1)/(C*N)
1040 PRINT USING 200:S
1050 STOP
1060 REM*************************************************
1070 REM
1080 REM           DRAW A CIRCLE WITH RADIUS, R
1090 REM
1100 REM*************************************************
1110 MOVE X1+R,Y1
1120 FOR Z=0 TO 360 STEP 10
1130 X2=R*COS(Z)
1140 Y2=R*SIN(Z)
1150 DRAW X1+X2,Y1+Y2
1160 NEXT Z
1170 RETURN
1180 REM*************************************************
```

Fig. 7.19 Torpedo game program (cont'd)

Chapter Eight

THE SPLIT LEVEL HOME (IDEAS)

"The first time I visited them I couldn't believe my eyes. Their house bulged with electronic equipment of every description. Computers monitored the household energy flow, security, maintenance, and entertainment facilities. We played a game of galactic proportions cast upon the south wall of the living room and drank from glasses filled by an automatic bar."

From the other side of the tracks

8.1 Family Room Fun

George loved to play games—any kind of game. He always won at poker and was more fortunate than most gamblers when he went to Las Vegas.

So it was no real surprise to his wife when George announced his intentions of digging up the back lawn to make room for a bowling lane. The bulldozers came, the carpenters came, and the painters came to help George transform his family room into a bowling alley.

Naturally, George owned a personal computer. He also knew ahead of time that his personal computer would be useful as a score keeper. However, keeping score in bowling turned out to require a more difficult program than George had anticipated.

Each bowling frame allows one or two throws per player. If all ten pins are pushed over on the first throw, the player is said to have made a *strike*, which is worth 10 points *plus the sum of the points of the next two throws.* If the player knocks over 10 pins in two throws, he makes a *spare*, which is worth 10 points *plus the points of the next single throw.* A spare may total as much as 20 points, whereas a strike can add up to 30 points (three strikes in a row).

A computer program to compute the total score, given the pins knocked down in each frame, must be able to "look ahead" to the next one or two throws whenever a spare or strike occurs. We will isolate each special case as shown below.

First, assume that the score is made up of three arrays (an array in BASIC is a block of numbers; each single number of the block is accessed via an index called its *subscript*). The F(11) array stores the score obtained from the first ball thrown. The second ball thrown results in either zero (because of a strike or an error) or a score resulting from knocking over additional pins. The second score of each frame is stored in S(10). The final array of interest in the solution to this problem is T(10). The running total, that is, the sums of pins knocked down, strikes, and spares, is stored in T. Hence,

$$T(i) = F(i) + S(i);\ i = 1, 2, \ldots, 10$$

This formula for T (total score in frame i) is used regardless of the nature of F and S. In the case where F and S indicate a spare or a strike, the value of T must be augmented to get the correct value. Assuming that F(11) = 0 and S(i) = 0 for all i, we get the following algorithm for computing bowling scores.

1. *IS THIS THE LAST FRAME?*
   YES: IF i = 10 THEN T(10) = T(9) + F(10) + S(10) + F(11) STOP
2. *IS THIS THE FIRST FRAME?*
   NO: IF i > 1 THEN T(i) = T(i) + T(i-1)
3. *SPARE OR STRIKE?*
   SPARE: IF S(i) + F(i) = 10 THEN T(i) = T(i) + F(i+1)
   STRIKE: IF F(i) = 10 THEN . . .
   DO: *NEXT FRAME NOT A STRIKE*
   IF F(i+1) < 10 THEN T(i) = T(i) + S(i+1)
   OR: *NEXT FRAME A STRIKE, TOO*
   IF F(i+1) = 10 THEN T(i) = T(i) + F(i+2)

Let's take an example and follow through the calculations outlined in the algorithm. Suppose the score sheet looks like the partially played game in Fig. 8.1. Follow the steps of the algorithm using F and S from the sample score in Fig. 8.1.

T(1) = F(1) + S(1) = 8 (First frame, i = 1)

1. IS THIS THE LAST FRAME? NO.
2. IS THIS THE FIRST FRAME? YES.
3. SPARE OR STRIKE? NO.
   T(2) = F(2) + S(2) = 10 (Second frame, i = 2)

1. IS THIS THE LAST FRAME? NO.

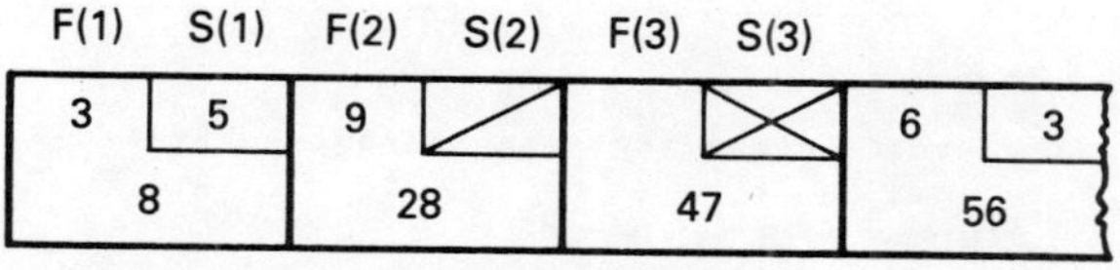

Fig. 8.1 Sample bowling score pad

2. IS THIS THE FIRST FRAME? NO.
   THEN T(2) = T(2) + T(1) = 18
3. SPARE OR STRIKE? SPARE.
   THEN T(2) = T(2) + F(3) = 18 + 10 = 28
   T(3) = F(3) + S(3) = 10 + 0 = 10 (Third frame, i = 3)

1. IS THIS THE LAST FRAME? NO.
2. IS THIS THE FIRST FRAME? NO.
   THEN T(3) = T(3) + T(2) = 38
3. SPARE OR STRIKE? STRIKE.
   THEN T(3) = T(3) + F(4) = 44
   NEXT FRAME NOT A STRIKE.
   THEN T(3) = T(3) + S(4) = 47
   T(4) = F(4) + S(4) = 9 (Fourth frame, i = 4)

1. IS THIS THE LAST FRAME? NO.
2. IS THIS THE FIRST FRAME? NO.
   THEN T(4) = T(4) + T(3) = 56
3. SPARE OR STRIKE? NO.

The algorithm continues to build the value of T(i) for each frame. In the last frame, we must remember to score a maximum of three throws (F(11)) in the event of a strike or spare.

The program shown in Fig. 8.2 straightforwardly implements a version of the bowling score calculator.

8.2 The Toy Room

Personal computers make great toys because they provide education as well as amusement. Examples of playing/teaching personal computers may be found in any school today.

A math drill program teaches children in the third grade how to type, read, and add numbers. Each problem is generated automatically using the INT (integer function) and the RND (random number function). For example, adding two numbers together, we have:

```
  INT(RND(0)*1000)
+ INT(RND(0)*1000)
= ________________
```

(A) Main Program

```
100 REM*********************************************
110 REM
120 REM      COMPUTE BOWLING SCORE
130 REM
140 REM*********************************************
150 REM
160 DIM F(11),S(10),T(10)
170 F(11)=0
180 REM
190 FOR I=1 TO 10
200 REM
210 REM---------------FIRST THROW---------------------
220 REM
230 PRINT USING 240:"ENTER FIRST BALL IN FRAME #",I;
240 IMAGE 27A,3D
250 INPUT F(I)
260 REM
270 REM------------GET SECOND THROW------------------
280 REM
290 LET S(I)=0
300 IF I=10 THEN 320
310 IF F(I)=10 THEN 380
320 PRINT USING 330:"ENTER SECOND BALL IN FRAME #",I;
330 IMAGE 28A,3D
340 INPUT S(I)
350 REM
360 REM------------TENTH FRAME ?---------------------
370 REM
380 IF I<10 THEN 430
390 IF F(I)+S(I)<10 THEN 430
400 PRINT USING 410:"ENTER THIRD BALL IN LAST FRAME ",I
410 IMAGE 31A,3D
420 INPUT F(11)
430 NEXT I
440 REM
450 REM---------------READY TO COMPUTE TOTALS---------
460 REM
470 GOSUB 490
480 STOP
```

(B) Actual Algorithm for Computing Bowling Scores

```
490 REM*********************************************
500 REM
510 REM        TALLY FRAMES
520 REM
530 REM*********************************************
540 REM
550 FOR I=1 TO 9
560 REM
570 REM--------------OPEN FRAME ---------------------
580 REM
590 LET T(I)=F(I)+S(I)
600 IF I=1 THEN 650
```

Fig. 8.2 Program for computing bowling scores

```
610 LET T(I)=T(I)+T(I-1)
620 REM
630 REM------------SPARE FRAME----------------------
640 REM
650 IF F(I)+S(I)<10 THEN 700
660 LET T(I)=T(I)+F(I+1)
670 REM
680 REM------------STRIKE FRAME----------------------
690 REM
700 IF F(I)<10 THEN 820
710 REM
720 REM-------------IS THERE TWO?---------------------
730 REM
740 IF F(I+1)=10 THEN 800
750 LET T(I)=T(I)+S(I+1)
760 GO TO 820
770 REM
780 REM ------------DOUBLE----------------------
790 REM
800 LET T(I)=T(I)+F(I+2)
810 REM
820 PRINT USING 830:"FRAME ",I," (",F(I),",",S(I),")","SCORE=",T(I)
830 IMAGE 6A,3D,3A,3D,1A,3D,1A,6A,4D
840 NEXT I
850 REM
860 LET I=10
870 LET T(10)=T(9)+F(11)+F(10)+S(10)
880 PRINT USING 830:"FRAME ",I," (",F(I),",",S(I),")","SCORE=",T(I)
890 PRINT
900 PRINT USING 910:"THE FINAL SCORE IS",T(10)
910 IMAGE 18A,5D
920 RETURN
```

Fig. 8.2 Program for computing bowling scores (cont'd)

The problem above produces three-digit numbers and checks the result. Since the computer can also store the scores of each student after each drill, the grading of papers is eliminated.

8.3 The Garden

A personal computer may communicate with analog devices (machines that measure continously rather than digitally). A *sample-and hold* interface provides the computer with an electronic device for measuring and digitizing voltages read from a thermostat, burglar alarm, etc.

Moisture content in the soil of a garden can be measured by an electronic device called a *transducer*. A transducer measures the electrical conductivity of wet ground, converts the measurement into electrical current, and transmits the current along a wire into a sample-and-hold interface. Thus, a personal computer can control (again through an interface and relays) the flow of water through a sprinkler system.

When a personal computer is connected to household and garden

```
DIAL    CALL  DISCON        DISCONNECT
        DE    1250          5 SECOND DELAY
        CALL  DELAY
        LA    COMADR        SET UP COMM BOX TO DIAL
        DI
        EX    ADR
        LA    030
        EX    COM1
        LA    0374          SET SPEED AT 100 BAUD
        EX    COM2
        EX    COM3
        LA    0377
        EX    COM2
        EX    COM3
        XRA
        EI
        EX    COM4
        DE    250
        CALL  DELAY         1 SECOND DELAY
        LC    0200
        CALL  WAITC         WAIT FOR DATA SET READY
        LA    COMADR
        DI
        EX    ADR
        LA    0230
        EI
        EX    COM1
        HL    RPHONE-1
NXDIG   CALL  INCHL
        CALL  SAVHL
        LAM
        CP    '*'
        JFZ   CMPR
        DE    500           WAIT 2 SECONDS IF *
        CALL  DELAY
        CALL  RESHL
        JMP   NXDIG
CMPR    CP    015
        JTZ   CONNECT
        CP    '9'+1
        JFS   NXDIG
        CP    '0'
        JTS   NXDIG
        JFZ   MASK
        LA    10
MASK    ND    017
        LBA
        LC    1
        CALL  WAITC         CHECK FOR TRANSMIT READY
NXOUT   LA    COMADR
        DI
        EX    ADR
        LA    0360
        EI
        EX    WRITE
```

Fig. 8.3 Telephone dial program in 8080 code

```
         LC     1
         CALL   WAITC              WAIT FOR TRANSMIT READY
         LAB
         SU     1
         LBA
         EX     CLICK
         JFZ    NXOUT
         DE     250                1 SECOND DELAY
         CALL   DELAY
         CALL   RESHL
         JMP    NXDIG
.
.  TEST FOR GOOD CONNECTION
.        CARRIER MUST COME UP WITHIN 20 SECONDS
.
CONNECT  LA     COMADR
         DI
         EX     ADR
         LA     0121
         EI
         EX     COM1
         LC     0200               WAIT FOR DATA COUPLER READY
         CALL   WAITC
         LC     200                WAIT 20 SECONDS FOR CARRIER
         CALL   TIME                 TO COME UP
         JFZ    SETUP              *SET UP FOR REMOTE OPERATION
```

Fig. 8.3 Telephone dial program (cont'd)

appliances, it can simulate the activities of a caretaker. While you are on vacation, the computer waters the garden and turns lights on and off; when you are home, it minimizes energy waste by varying the air conditioner throughout a hot summer day.

8.4 A Telephone Monitor

In order to show how a personal computer can be programmed to control standard household devices, we shall describe a telephone operating program. This program must be written in machine language in order to handle the telephone "caller," which is attached to a "modem." The modem converts signals into sound and sound back into signals so that we can communicate over audio telephone lines

The machine language routine can be called from BASIC (most versions of BASIC provide for it). If not, additional code will be needed to request telephone numbers, etc.

The 8080 code for automatically dialing a telephone number is shown in Fig. 8.3. Recall that an 8080 machine processes data by moving it from memory to one of seven 8-bit registers. The registers are lettered A, B, C, D, E, H, and L. In the programs of Fig. 8.3, we have used macros to load registers and register pairs.

For example, we often want to load HL as a pair because HL points to operands in main memory. Other macros are described below.

DE	operand:	Load constant or address into DE
HL	operand:	Load constant or address into HL
LAM	:	Load A with a number from M (main memory). The address of M is assumed to be in HL
LBA	:	Copy contents of A into register B
LAB	:	Copy register B into register A

The programs also use machine language tricks, for example:

XRA	clears register A (set to zeros)
ND 017	clears left four bits of register A

The programs use functions defined outside the code given. These functions provide useful communications operations, ease in programming the (Ackward) 8080, and readability.

DISCON	This subroutine disconnects the telephone from the communications modem. It is used to reinitialize before attempting to dial a new number.
DELAY	This subroutine delays the computer by decrementing the DE register pair.
WAIT C	This subroutine delays the computer by waiting for a signal from the modem. It differs from DELAY because it waits an unspecified length of time (until a "READY" signal is received).
INCHL	Increments the HL register pair.
SAVHL	Saves the HL register pair.
RESHL	Restores the HL register pair.
TIME	Waits for a carrier to come up.

In addition to these functions, the routines of Fig. 8.3 use symbolic addresses and constants to make the program readable. These addresses and constants are defined as follows:

COMADR	Address of the communications (modem and direct access arrangement box). Interface that links the 8080 with the telephone.
ADR	Used in an external command to indicate that the I/O is sent out over an address line instead of a data line.
COM 1,2,3	Send control signals to the communication box as opposed to sending data. Various COMs are used to control the box.

RPHONE	The address of the phone number being dialed.
WRITE	Sends data to the telephone.
CLICK	Dials a click. Three clicks are sent when dialing a 3, five for dialing a 5, etc. When a zero is dialed, 10 clicks are sent.

Now that we understand the code used in Fig. 8.3, we can briefly describe the program and its actions. We assume a hardware configuration that provides autodialing over a DAA (Direct-Access Arrangement), as provided by the telephone company. Such a DAA and COM box require codes which we avoid explaining in great detail by using COM1, COM2, etc.

Lines 1046–1049 initialize the DIAL routine by disconnecting, waiting five seconds for the telephone to adjust to a "hang-up," and then commanding the communications box to redial. The DI command in line 1050 disables all interrupts so that no interference from other processes going on in the machine are permitted.

Lines 1051–1060 send codes to the interface telling it to begin sending clicks at the rate of 100 baud (about 10 characters per second, or teletype speed). The interrupts are enabled again in line 1061.

Lines 1062–1067 cause the computer to wait for a carrier signal indicating that the telephone is ready to dial. Lines 1068–1073 acknowledge that the carrier is received, and give final notice to the COM box that dialing is to begin.

In NXDIG at lines 1074–1094, the next digit (obtained through pointer RPHONE, which gives the address of the telephone number stored in main memory) is read, examined, and then dialed by routine NXOUT. Line 1077 checks to see if the number has an asterisk in it. If so, the dialer delays 2 seconds. This is used for delaying between an area code and the remaining number. For example, 503*2584195 would dial the area code, wait 2 seconds after the 503, and then dial the remaining digits.

Lines 1083–1090 in CMPR make sure that the telephone number has digits only. If other characters are found, they are either ignored, or the system examines the line to see if the carrier is still coming in (CONNECT).

The telephone number stored at RPHONE is an ASCII string containing zone bits in the high-order four bits of each 8-bit byte. The zone bits are stripped off by MASK at lines 1091–1093. Finally, we are ready to actually dial the digit in line 1095 (NXOUT).

Lines 1095–1107 check to make sure that the last CLICK was sent out and then send another CLICK. When D clicks have been sent out by repeating lines 1095–1107 D times for digit D, the routine waits 1 second and returns to get another digit. Register B holds digit D while this is going on. Notice that in lines 1103–1104, the value of D is decremented (SU is a subtract) and then tested for zero in line 1107.

The autodial routine illustrated here is one of many routines needed to connect a personal computer to a telephone. Combining a telephone, tape recorder, and computer offers interesting possibilities in automated answering services and message referral.

8.5 Making Music

Personal computers make excellent controllers for sound productions. The high-speed output of ones and zeros in the form of tones can be input to the preamplifier of any stereo to produce artificial sound. Since the sound may be "tinny," it is often shaped before being sent out to the speakers.

Shaping sound signals requires expensive analog synthesizers or very high-speed digital computers. Both alternatives are impractical for most home hobbyists.

Another approach to making music is called "memory interference." Operation of a computer near a radio often causes "static" because of the field emission of the computer's memory. This static can be controlled to produce reasonable sound.

A variety of methods exist for producing sound with a computer. They offer an opportunity for experimentation between human beings and machines in a totally new way.

The score of Fig. 8.4(A) can be translated into the BASIC language of Fig. 8.4(B). A personal computer can then translate a program of this sort into computer signals and input them to the preamplifier of a stereo.

Every song consists elementally of parts, measures, and notes and is arranged for one or more voices. In Fig. 8.4, the score for a treble clef tune is shown to consist of a single part (called part A), three measures, and five notes and is set for a single voice.

Statement 10 is a comment (/) indicating the name of the tune. Lines 20 and 30 set the speed of the generator at 100 beats for every quarter note and assign K1 as the key with one sharp.

Part A is designated by line 40 and extends to line 70. Part B is a repeat of part A (see line 80).

In each of the lines 50 through 70, the score is divided into measures, M1, M2, M3. The first measure is in treble clef (*) for only one voice, V1. The notes are numbered from zero (middle C) to 15. Thus, the first quarter note is number 5. The second note is a dotted quarter note, number 6, as is the final note, number 9.

The second measure consists of a single voice in treble clef with one whole note, number 2. The final note in measure 3 (M3) is a whole note (number 7).

Line 80 causes part A to be repeated. The score is "executed" by

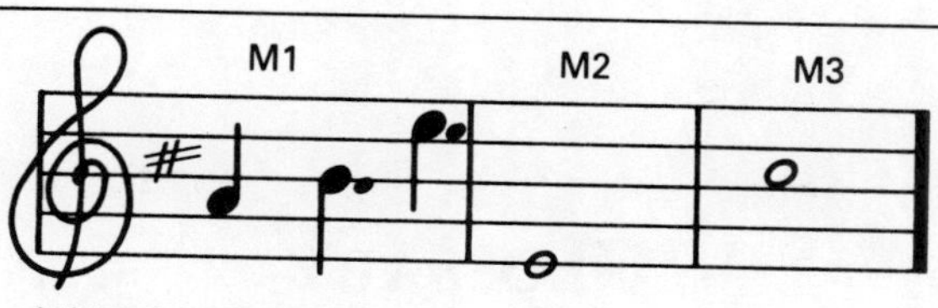

(A) Treble Clef tune

```
10    /  TREBLE CLEF TUNE
20    NQ = 100
30    K1
40    PA
50    M1   * V1   Q5   Q.6   9
60    M2   * V1   W2
70    M3   * V1   W7
80    PB   RA
```

(B) Computer language score for the tune in (A)

Fig. 8.4 Example of a music generator

converting it to electrical signals that oscillate at an audible frequency and are converted by any stereo into sound.

Most personal computers are thus capable of producing an almost endless number of musical variations. We leave the exploration of such variations to the reader.

GLOSSARY

absolute address A number that is permanently assigned as the address of a storage location.

access time The time required to locate a storage location.

accumulator A register in which the result of an operation is formed.

ACK/NAK A positive or negative response by a receiving terminal to indicate whether or not a block of data has been received correctly.

acoustic coupler A form of modem that sends and receives data as tones over a telephone line using a conventional telephone handset.

address A label, name, or number that designates a location where information is stored.

algorithm A prescribed set of well-defined rules or processes for the solution of a problem in a finite number of steps.

alphanumeric Pertaining to a character set that contains both letters and numerals and usually other characters.

argument (1) A variable or constant that is given in the call of a subroutine as information to it. (2) A variable upon whose value the value of a function depends. (3) The known reference factor necessary to find an item in a table or array (that is, the index).

arithmetic unit The component of a computer where arithmetic and logical operations are performed.

ARQ An error control technique in which the receiving station responds with a "NAK" character if a message is received in error. The NAK is interpreted by the sending station as an Automatic Repeat Request.

array An arrangement of elements into one or more dimensions. A one-dimensional array is commonly called a *vector*; a two-dimensional array is called a *table* or a *matrix*.

ASCII An abbreviation for American Standard Code for Information Interchange.

ASR A designation used to indicate the Automatic Send and Receive capabilities of teletypes equipped with punched-tape equipment.

assemble To translate from a symbolic program to a binary program by substituting binary operation codes for symbolic operation codes and absolute or relocatable addresses for symbolic addresses.

assembler A program that translates symbolic op-codes into machine language and assigns memory locations for variables and constants.

asynchronous transmission A mode of transmission using start and stop bits to frame a character (hence, frequently called "Start/Stop transmission"). Although bits within a character occur at well-defined intervals, they are not as precisely timed as in synchronous transmission, and characters do not recur at any predictable interval.

atom The elementary building block of data structures. An atom corresponds to a record in a file and may contain one or more fields of data. Also called *node.*

audio response unit A unit used in "voice answer back" applications and digitally controlled to produce syllable and word responses to persons entering keyboard data.

auto-indexing Indexing in which, when addressed indirectly, the content of a location is incremented by one rewritten in the same location and used as the effective address of the current instruction.

autopolling Performing the polling function automatically to reduce the data communication tasks of the host computer. Autopolling can be performed by communication preprocessors, multiplexors, data concentrators, and the like.

autorestart A capability of a computer to perform automatically the initialization functions necessary to resume operation following an equipment or power failure.

auxiliary memory Data storage other than main memory; for example, storage on magnetic tape or direct-access devices.

auxiliary storage Storage that supplements main memory, such as disk or tape.

average The statistical mean; the expected value.

average search length The expected number of comparisons needed to locate an item in a data structure.

backtracking The operation of scanning a list in reverse.

backward pointer A pointer which gives the location of an atom's predecessor.

balanced sort An external tape sort that sorts by merging together tapes, each with an equal number of strings.

bandwidth A measure of the ability of equipment or transmission links to pass a range of frequencies.

base address A given address from which an absolute address is derived by combination with a relative address; synonymous with *address constant.*

batch processing A mode of data processing which processes one job after another in some order.

baud The maximum rate of transmission of signal elements; usually equivalent to bits per second.

baudot code A specific code using five bits to represent a character.

BCD code A specific code using six bits to represent a character, based on the Binary Coded Decimal representation of the decimal digits 0 through 9.

binary Pertaining to the number system with a radix of two.

binary code A code that makes use of exactly two distinct characters, 0 and 1.

binary radix sort A radix sort in which the sort radix is 2.

binary search A search method which begins with the middle element, discards half the list and repeats on the sublist until a matching key is found or until dividing the list produces an empty list.

binary search tree A binary search accomplished by storing the list in a binary tree. The tree is ordered when constructed or when insertions are made in order to facilitate the search.

binary tree A tree in which each node has an outdegree of at most 2.

bit A unit of information either zero or one (derived from a binary digit).

block A set of consecutive machine words, characters, or digits handled as a unit, particularly with reference to I/O.

block search To accomplish a block search, determine the block the item might be in; then linearly search the block.

bootstrap A technique or device designed to bring a program into the computer from an input device.

BPS Bits Per Second

branch A point in a routine where one of two or more choices is made under control of the routine.

break A communication circuit interruption, frequently used by the receiving terminal to interrupt the transmitting terminal.

broadcast The transmission of a message intended for all receiving terminals connected to the communication channel.

BROM Bipolar Read-Only Memory, a read-only memory using large-scale integration (LSI) bipolar devices.

BSC An IBM designation meaning "Binary Synchronous Communication" and referring to a specific communications procedure using synchronous data transmission.

bubble sort A sort achieved by exchanging pairs of keys, which begins with the first pair and exchanges successive pairs until the list is ordered; also called *ripple sort.*

buffer A storage space used to store I/O data temporarily.

buffered I/O A method of overlapping I/O using two or more buffers.

bug A mistake in the design or implementation of a program resulting in erroneous results.

byte A group of binary digits usually operated upon as a unit.

call To transfer control to a specified routine.

calling sequence A specified set of instructions and data necessary to set up and call a given routine.

cascade sort An external tape sort that sorts by merging strings from all but one tape onto the remaining tape. Subsequent passes merge fewer tapes until one tape contains all items.

central processing unit The unit of a computing system that includes the circuits controlling the interpretation and execution of instructions, that is, the computer proper, excluding I/O and other peripheral devices.

channel, communications A facility for communicating information; also called a *link, line, circuit, data path*, and the like.

character A single letter, numeral, or symbol used to represent information.

character checking The checking of each character by examining all characters as a group or field.

character template A device used to shape an electron beam into an alphanumeric character for CRT display.

circular list A linked list in which the last element points to the first one; also called *ring.*

clear To erase the contents of a storage location by replacing the contents, normally with zeros or spaces; to set to zero.

clear to send An EIA RS–232–C designation applied to a sense circuit used by a terminal or computer to detect whether its modem is ready to send data.

clock A device for timing events. In data communications, a clock is required to control the timing of bits sent in a data stream and to control the timing of the sampling of bits received in a data stream.

cluster *See* Primary cluster; Secondary cluster.

code A specific relationship between a set of bit patterns and a set of characters.

code level The number of bits used to represent a character (for example, the five-bit baudot code is a "five-level code").

coding To write instructions for a computer using symbols meaningful to the computer, or to an assembler, compiler, or other language processor.

collision An act that occurs when two or more keys hash to the same address.

column-major order A method of storing a two-dimensional array in which all elements in one column are placed before all elements in the next column. This method can also be used to store higher-dimensional arrays.

command A user order to a computer system, usually given through a keyboard.

compaction Packing of data structure to make room in memory.

comparative sort A sort by comparison of two or more keys.

compatibility The ability of an instruction or source language to be used on more than one computer.

compile To produce a binary-coded program from a program written in source (symbolic) language by selecting appropriate subroutines from a subroutine library, as directed by the instructions or other symbols of the source program. The linkage is supplied for combining the subroutines into a workable program, and the subroutine and linkage are translated into binary code.

compiler A program which translates statements and formulas written in a source language into a machine language program, for example, a FORTRAN compiler. Such a program usually generates more than one machine instruction for each statement.

complement *One's complement:* To replace all 0 bits with 1 bits and vice versa. *Two's complement:* To form the one's complement and add 1.

completeness check A check that verifies that no fields are missing and that no part of the record has been skipped in sequence.

concatenation The joining together of two or more strings to form a new one.

conditional assembly Assembly of certain parts of a symbolic program only if certain conditions have been met.

conditional skip Transfer of control to another point in the program depending upon whether a condition within the program is met.

connected graph A graph in which it is possible to get from one node to any other node along a sequence of edges. If the graph is directed, the direction of the edges may be disregarded.

connection matrix *See* incidence matrix.

consistency check A check in which two or more pieces of data are considered in relation to each other.

console Usually the external front side of a device where controls and indicators are available for manual operation of the device.

contiguous data structure *See* Sequential data structure.

control character A character inserted into a data stream with the intent of signaling the receiving station to perform some function.

control totals Totals taken on amount fields or quantity fields of like sizes, such as units, dozens, or cases. These totals are added algebraically.

convert (1) To change numerical data from one radix to another. (2) To transfer data from one recorded format to another.

count The successive increase or decrease of a cumulative total of the number of times an event occurs.

counter A register or storage location (variable) used to represent the number of occurrences of an operation (*see* Loop).

CPS Characters Per Second

CPU Central Processing Unit

CRC A method of error detection using Cyclic Redundancy Check characters. A CRC character, generated at the transmitting terminal, is based on the contents of the message transmitted. A similar CRC generation is performed at the receiving terminal. If the two characters match, the message was probably received correctly.

crossfooting checks Cross-adding or subtracting two or more fields and zero-balancing the result against the original result. This is an effective control when total debits, total credits, and a balance-forward amount are maintained in each account; total debits and total credits can be crossfooted to prove that the difference equals the balance forward.

CRT A Cathode Ray Tube used to display information.

current location counter A counter kept by an assembler to determine the address that has been assigned to either an instruction or constant being assembled.

cursor A position indicator frequently employed in a display on a video terminal to indicate a character to be corrected or a position in which data is to be entered.

cycle A path which starts and terminates at the same node.

cycle time The length of time it takes the computer to reference one word of memory.

cyclic redundancy check *See* CRC.

cylinder The tracks of a disk storage device that can be accessed without repositioning the access mechanism.

data A general term used to denote any or all facts, numbers, letters, and symbols. It connotes basic elements of information which can be processed or produced by a computer.

data modem A modulation/demodulation device that enables computers and terminals to communicate over telephone circuits.

dataphone An AT&T designation for a service which provides data communication over telephone facilities.

data set Another term for *modem.*

data structure The relationship between data items.

date check A check the primary purpose of which is to ensure that the record date is acceptable.

DDD An abbreviation for Direct Distance Dialing, the facility used for making long-distance telephone calls without the assistance of a telephone operator. DDD is frequently used to mean the switched telephone network.

debug To detect, locate, and correct mistakes in a program.

delimiter A character that separates, terminates, and organizes elements of a statement or program.

demodulation A process for deriving information from a modulated carrier.

dense list A list stored in contiguous locations; also called *linear list, sequential list.*

density The ratio of the number of information bits to the total number of bits in a structure.

deque A double-ended queue that allows insertions and deletions at both ends of a list.

device flags One-bit registers that record the current status of a device.

digit A character used to represent one of the nonnegative integers smaller than the radix; for example, in binary notation, either 0 or 1.

digital computer A device that operates on discrete data, performing sequences of arithmetic and logical operations on this data.

digraph *See* Directed graph.

direct address An address that specifies the location of an instruction.

directed graph A set of nodes and edges in which an initial and a terminal node determine the direction of the edge. An edge from node A to node B is not an edge from node B to node A.

directory A partition by software into several distinct files; a directory of these files is maintained on a device to locate the files.

display register An internal register in a CRT display terminal.

distributive sort A sort achieved by partitioning a list and then exchanging items until order exists between partitioned sublists.

division checking Division is usually checked by multiplication, that is, by multiplying the quotient by the divisor, adding the remainder, and zero-balancing the result against the original dividend.

dope vector An atom of a linked list that describes the contents of subsequent atoms in the list.

double precision Pertaining to the use of two computer words to represent one number.

doubly linked list A linked list in which each atom contains two pointer fields, one of which points to the atom's successor and the other to the atom's predecessor.

dummy Used as an adjective to indicate an artificial address, instruction, or record of information inserted solely to fulfill prescribed conditions, as in a "dummy" variable.

dump To copy the contents of all or part of memory, usually onto an external storage medium.

duplex channel A communication channel with the capability of simultaneous two-way communication; equivalent to *full-duplex.*

dynamic memory management system A memory system that supplies a variably sized space depending upon the request.

EBCDIC code A specific code using eight bits to represent a character. The abbreviation stands for Extended Binary Coded Decimal Interchange Code.

echo check An error control technique wherein the receiving terminal or computer returns the original message to the sender to verify that the message was received correctly.

echo-plex A communication procedure wherein characters keyboarded by the operator do not print directly on his printer but are sent to a computer that echoes the characters back for printing. This procedure, requiring full-duplex communication facilities, provides a form of error control by displaying to the operator an indication of the character received by the computer.

edge A connection between two nodes in a graph; it may or may not have direction.

editor *See* Symbolic editor.

effective address The address actually used in the execution of a computer instruction.

EIA Electronic Industries Association.

empty string A string containing no characters (of length zero); also called *null string.*

EOB End of Block.

EOM End of Message.

error control A plan, implemented by hardware, software, procedures, and the like, to detect and/or correct errors introduced into a data communications system.

error transmission A change in data resulting from the transmission process.

execute To carry out an instruction or run a program on the computer.

external fragmentation Memory loss caused by checkerboarding.

external sort A sort performed while all or part of a list is stored on an auxiliary storage device.

external storage A separate facility or device on which data usable by the computer is stored (such as paper tape, magnetic tape, or disk).

fail soft A method of system implementation designed to prevent the irretrievable loss of facilities or data in the event of a temporary outage of some portion of the system.

field A unit of information.

field checking Checking concerned with the contents of fields within records.

FIFO First In, First Out queue discipline.

file A collection of related records treated as a unit.

file-structured device A device such as disk or tape which contains records organized into files and accessible through file names found in a directory file; see Directory.

filename Alphanumeric characters used to identify a particular file.

filename extension A short appendage to the filename used to identify the type of data in the file; for example, BIN signifying a binary program.

filial set A collection of "sons" descended from a particular node in a tree.

firmware That portion of control-memory hardware which can be tailored to create microprograms for a user-oriented instruction set.

fixed point The position of the radix point of a number system; this position is constant according to a predetermined convention.

flag A variable or register used to record the status of a program or device; in the latter case, also called a *device flag.*

flip-flop A device with two stable states.

floating point A number system in which the position of the radix point is indicated by one part of the number (the *exponent*) and another part represents the significant digits (the *mantissa*).

flowchart A graphical representation of the operations required to carry out a data processing operation.

forest A collection of trees.

format The arrangement of data.

forward pointer A pointer that tells the location of the next item in a data structure.

four-out-of-eight-code A communication code which facilitates error detection because four of the eight bits representing a character are always marking.

fragmentation Loss of usable memory as a result of checkerboarding or mismatch in fit. *See* Internal fragmentation; External fragmentation.

frequency The rate of recurrence of some cyclic or repetitive event, such as the rate of repetition of a sine-wave electrical current; usually expressed in cycles per second, or Hertz.

frequency division multiplexing The merging of several signals of lesser bandwidth into a composite signal for transmission over a communication channel of greater bandwidth. Example: five signals with a bandwidth of 100 Hz each might be accommodated on a channel having a bandwidth of 500 Hz.

full duplex Descriptive of a communications channel capable of simultaneous and independent transmission and reception.

function subprogram A subprogram that returns a single value result, usually in the accumulator.

garbage collection Release of unused portions of memory from a data structure to make unused areas of memory available for use.

graph A set containing two elements: nodes and edges. It provides a mathematical model for data structures in which the nodes correspond to data items and the edges to pointer fields.

half duplex Descriptive of a communications channel capable of transmission and/or reception, but not both simultaneously.

handshaking A preliminary procedure performed by modems and/or terminals and computers to verify that communication has been established and can proceed.

hardware Physical equipment, for example, mechanical, electrical, or electronic devices.
hash totals A hash total is the sum of the digits of an identifying field.
hashing A key-to-address transformation in which the keys determine the location of the data.
head A special data item that points to the beginning of a list. A device that reads or writes data on a storage medium.
header That part of a message preceding the text, frequently specifying message destination, source, priority, and the like.
heap sort *See* Tree sort.
hexadecimal system A numbering system with 16 admissable combinations represented by the symbols 0 through 9 and A through F.
Hollerith code A specific code using twelve levels of a punched card to represent a character.
horizontal distribution A method of assigning initial strings to tapes when employing the polyphase sort.
Huffman tree A minimal value tree; *see* Minimal tree; Optimal merge tree.

incidence matrix A two-dimensional array that describes the edges in a graph. Also called *connection matrix.*
indegree The number of directed edges that point to a node.
index A symbol or numeral that locates the position of an item in an array.
indirect address An address in a computer instruction that indicates a location where the address of the referenced operand is to be found.
infix notation A notation where operators are embedded within operands.
initialize To set counters, switches, and addresses to zero or other starting values at the beginning of, or at prescribed points in, a computer routine.
instruction A command which causes the computer or system to perform an operation; usually one line of a program.
intelligent terminal A terminal with some level of programmable "intelligence" for performing preprocessing or postprocessing operations.
interactive A system that performs processing or problem-solving tasks by carrying on a dialogue with the user.
interface A well-defined boundary, such as the interface between a modem and a terminal, or the interface between a communications controller and a computer's I/O bus.
internal fragmentation Memory loss caused by a mismatch between available space and the requested size of space.
internal sort A sort made while all items remain in main memory.
internal storage The storage facilities forming an integral physical part of the computer and directly controlled by the computer. Also called main memory and core memory.
interpreter A program that translates and executes source language statements at run-time.
I/O Abbreviation for Input/Output.
IRG Inter-Record Gap.
iteration Repetition of a group of instructions.

job A unit of code which solves a problem, that is, a program and all its related subroutines and data.

jump A departure from the normal sequence of executing instructions in a computer.

K An abbreviation for the prefix *kilo*, that is, 1024 in decimal notation.

key One or more fields in a record that is used to locate the record or control its use.

key to address *See* Hashing.

KSR A designation used to indicate the Keyboard Send and Printer Receive capabilities of teletypes and comparable equipment.

label One or more characters used to identify a source language statement or line.

language, assembly The machine-oriented programming language used by an assembly system.

language, computer A systematic means of communicating instructions and information to the computer.

language, machine Information that can be directly processed by the computer; expressed in binary notation.

language, source A computer language in which programs are first written and which require extensive translation in order to be executed by the computer.

leaf A terminal node of a tree.

least significant digit The right-most digit of a number.

level A measure of the distance from a node to the root of a tree.

library routines A collection of standard routines which can be incorporated into larger programs.

LIFO Last In, First Out stack discipline.

limit check A limit check places upper or lower quantitative limits on a field.

line feed The teletype operation which advances the paper by one line.

line number In source languages such as BASIC and FORTRAN, a number which begins a line of the source program for purposes of identification; a numeric label.

linear list *See* Dense list.

linear search A search which begins with the first element and compares until a matching key is found or the end of the list is reached.

link (1) A one-bit register in most computers. (2) An address pointer to the next element of a list or the next record of a file.

linkage The code that connects two separately coded routines.

linked list A list in which each atom contains a pointer to the location of the next atom.

list An ordered collection of atoms.

literal A symbol which defines itself.

load To place data or programs into internal storage.

location A place in storage or memory where a unit of data or an instruction may be stored.

longitudinal redundancy check A method of error detection using a parity bit for each level in the code being transmitted. Following a block of characters, an LRC character is inserted to make the number of bits transmitted on each of the code levels either odd or even. To check the accuracy of the received data, an LRC character is generated by the receiving terminal and compared with the LRC character received from the transmitting terminal.

loop A sequence of instructions that is executed repeatedly until a terminal condition prevails.

LRC Longitudinal Redundancy Check.

machine language programming This term is used to mean the actual binary machine instructions.

macro instruction An instruction in a source language that is equivalent to a specified sequence of machine instructions.

main memory The main high-speed storage of a computer in which binary data is represented by the switching of MOS transistors.

manual input The entry of data by hand into a device at the time of processing.

manual operation The processing of data in a system by direct manual techniques.

mark The state of a communication channel corresponding to a binary one. The marking condition exists when current flows (hole in paper tape) on a current-loop channel, or when the voltage is more negative than −3 volts on an EIA RS-232-C channel.

mask A bit pattern which selects those bits from a word of data which are to be used in some subsequent operation.

masking A technique for sensing specific binary conditions and ignoring others. Typically accomplished by placing zeros in bit positions of no interest, and ones in bit positions to be sensed.

mass storage Pertaining to a device such as disk or tape which stores large amounts of data readily accessible to the central processing unit.

matrix A rectangular array of elements; any table can be considered a matrix.

memory (1) The alterable storage in a computer. (2) Pertaining to a device in which data can be stored and from which it can be retrieved.

memory protection A method of preventing the contents of some part of main memory from being destroyed or altered.

merge sort A sort that merges ordered sublists to form a larger ordered list.

message A group of characters communicated as a unit, typically including a HEADER, TEXT, ERROR CONTROL, and END-OF-MESSAGE indication.

microprogram A series of microcommands assembled to perform a specific function.

minimal tree A tree with terminal nodes so placed that the value of the tree is optimal; *see* Optimal merge tree.

modem A modulation/demodulation device that enables computers and terminals to communicate over telephone circuits.

modulation A process for impressing information on a carrier.

monitor The master control program that observes, supervises, controls, or verifies the operation of a system.

most significant digit The left-most nonzero digit.
multi-drop circuit A communication system configuration using a single channel or line to serve multiple terminals.
multilinked list A list in which each atom has two or more pointers.
multiplex In communications applications, the concurrent transmission of more than one information stream on a single channel.
multiprocessing Utilization of several computers or processors to divide jobs or processes logically or functionally and to execute them simultaneously.
multiprogramming Pertains to the execution of two or more programs in main memory at the same time. Execution switches between programs.

nesting (1) Including a program loop inside another loop. (2) Algebraic nesting, such as (A+B*(C+D)), where execution proceeds from the innermost to the outermost level.
network The interconnection of multiple communication channels and multiple terminals and/or computers.
nil pointer A pointer used to denote the end of a linked list.
node *See* Atom.
noise Signals bearing no desired information and frequently capable of introducing errors into the communication process.
NOP An instruction that specifically does nothing (control proceeds to the next instruction in the sequence).
normalize To adjust the exponent and mantissa of a floating-point number so that the mantissa appears in a prescribed format.
null string A string containing no characters; also called *empty string.*

object program The binary coded program that constitutes the output after translation of a source language program.
octal Pertaining to the number system with a radix of 8.
off-line Pertaining to equipment or devices not under direct control of the computer and to the processes performed on such devices.
on-line Pertaining to equipment or devices under direct control of the computer and to programs that respond immediately to user commands.
operand (1) A quantity which is affected, manipulated, or operated upon. (2) The address, or symbolic name, portion of an assembly language instruction.
operating system A set of programs controlling the operation of a data processing system.
operator The symbol or code that indicates an action (or operation) to be performed.
optimal merge tree A tree representation of the order in which strings are to be merged so that a minimum number of move operations occurs.
OR *Inclusive OR:* A logical operation such that the result is true if either or both operands are true, and false if both operands are false. *Exclusive OR:* A logical operation such that the result is true if either operand is true, and false if both operands are either true or false. When neither case is specifically indicated, inclusive OR is assumed; *see also* Inclusive OR and Exclusive OR.

origin The absolute address of the beginning of a section of code.

oscillating sort An external tape sort which capitalizes on a tape drive's ability to read forward and backward. The sort oscillates between an internal sort and an external merge.

outdegree The number of directed edges leaving a node.

output Information transferred from the internal storage of a computer to output devices or external storage.

overflow An act that occurs if the allotted memory for a data structure is exceeded.

pad character A character inserted to fill a blank time slot in synchronous transmission, or inserted to fulfill a character-count requirement in transmissions of fixed block lengths.

page A section of main memory.

parallel transmission The simultaneous transmission of all bits comprising a single character.

parity A method of error detection using an extra bit to make the total number of marking bits in a character either odd or even. If a character is sent with odd parity, it should be received with odd parity if no errors are introduced by the communication process.

parity check The examination of a character and its parity bit to determine if the character has been received correctly.

parsing The process of separating statements into syntactic units.

pass One complete cycle during which a body of data is processed. An assembler usually requires two passes during which a source program is translated into binary code.

patch To modify a routine in a rough or expedient way.

path A path from node n_i to node n_j that is, a set of nodes n_i, n_{i+1}, . . . , n_{j-1}, n_j and edges such that there is an edge between successive pairs of nodes.

peripheral equipment In a data processing system, any unit of equipment, distinct from the central processing unit, which may provide the system with outside storage or communication.

pointer An address or other indication of location.

pointer address Address of a memory location containing the actual (effective) address of desired data.

polling The regular and systematic interrogation of terminals to determine if a terminal has messages awaiting transmission, and to determine the state of readiness of a terminal to accept messages.

polyphase sort An external tape sort which works best with six or fewer tapes. A Fibonacci sequence of merges is established that maintains a maximum number of active tapes throughout the sort.

pop The act of removing an element from a stack; also called *pull.*

postfix notation A notation in which operators follow the operands that they operate on.

primary cluster A buildup of table entries around a single table-location.

priority interrupt An interrupt which is given preference over other interrupts within the system.

procedure The course of action taken for the solution of a problem; see also *Algorithm.*

program The complete sequence of instructions and routines necessary to solve a problem.

PROM Programmable Read-Only Memory; a semiconductor diode array that is programmed by fusing or burning out diode junctions.

protocol A set of procedures or conventions used routinely between equipment such as terminals and computers.

pseudo-operation An instruction to the assembler; an operation code that is not part of the computer's hardware command repertoire.

pull *See* Pop.

push The act of placing an element on a stack; also called *put.*

pushdown list A list that is constructed and maintained so that the next item to be retrieved is the item most recently stored in the list.

put *See* Push.

quadratic quotient search A hashing algorithm that uses a quadratic offset when probing subsequent table locations.

queue A list that allows insertion of atoms at one end and deletion of atoms at the opposite end.

queuing A method of controlling the information processing sequence.

quickersort A sort performed by partitioning a list into two sublists and a pivotal middle element. All items greater than the pivot go in one sublist and all lesser items go in the other sublist. Sublists are further subdivided until all items are ordered.

radix The base of a number system; the number of digit symbols required by a number system.

radix sort A distributive sort that uses a number of partitions equal to the sort radix.

random access A method of retrieving data from a secondary storage device in which the retrieval time is independent of the location of the data; contrast with Sequential access.

range check A range check is usually applied to a code in order to verify that it falls within a given set of characters or numbers.

read To transfer information from an input device to memory.

real-time Pertaining to a computation performed while the related physical process is taking place so that results of the computation can be used in guiding the physical process.

reasonableness check A programmed judgment on data to determine whether it is normal.

record A collection of related data items (a collection of related records makes up a *file.*

recursion A reactivation of an active process; for example, a program segment which calls itself.

recursive subroutine A subroutine capable of calling itself.

redundancy A repetition of information or the insertion of information which is not new, and therefore redundant. Example: the use of check bits and check characters in data communication is a form of redundancy; hence the terms: cyclic redundancy, longitudinal redundancy, vertical redundancy.

redundancy check The use of redundancy to check errors; *see* CRC, LRC, VRC.

register A device capable of storing a specified amount of data, usually one word.

relative address The number that specifies the difference between the actual address and a base address.

relocatable Descriptive of a routine whose instructions are written so that they can be located and executed in different parts of main memory.

remote Physically distant from a local computer, terminal, multiplexor, and the like.

replacement-selection A tournament method of sorting tape files that produces ordered strings of various lengths which must be merged.

response time Time between initiating an operation from a remote terminal and obtaining the result (including transmission time to and from the computer, processing time, and access time for the files employed).

restart To resume execution of a program.

ring *See* Circular list.

ripple sort *See* Bubble sort.

RJE An IBM designation meaning Remote Job Entry and referring to the programs used to submit processing jobs from terminals.

RO A designation used to indicate the Receive Only capabilities of teletypes and other equipment lacking keyboards and paper-tape equipment.

ROM A Read Only Memory system wherein the stored bit patterns cannot be rewritten or otherwise altered.

root The node with indegree zero.

routine A set of instructions arranged in proper sequence so that the computer can perform a desired task; a program or subprogram.

row-major order A method of storing a two-dimensional array in which all elements in one row are placed before all elements in the next row; *see also* Column-major order.

RS–232 A technical specification published by the Electronic Industries Association establishing the interface requirements between modems and terminals or computers.

run A single, continuous execution of a program.

scan An algorithmic procedure for visiting or listing each node of a data structure.

scatter storage *See* Hashing.

secondary cluster A build-up along a path established by a pattern in a hashing function used for table look-up.

segment (1) That part of a long program which may be resident in main memory at any one time. (2) To divide a program into two or more segments or to store part of a routine on an external storage device so that it may be brought into main memory as needed.

selection sort A sort that selects the extreme value (largest or smallest) in a list, exchanges it with the last value in the list, and repeats with a shorter list.

self-checking number A self-checking number is one that has a precalculated digit appended to the basic number for the purpose of catching keypunch or transmission errors.

sequence check A check performed if incoming data records must be sequenced for further processing. If applicable, this type of check can be expanded to include a check on multiple records making up one transaction.

sequential access An access method for storing or retrieving data items which are located in a continuous manner. The retrieval time of an item depends in part on how many items precede it.

sequential data structure A data structure in which each atom is immediately adjacent to the next atom; also called *contiguous data structure.*

sequential list *See* Dense list.

sequential search *See* Linear search.

serial access Pertaining to the sequential or consecutive transmission of data to or from memory, as with paper tape; contrast with Random access.

serial transmission The transmission of the bits of a character in sequence, one at a time.

shift A movement of bits to the left or right that is frequently performed in the accumulator.

simplex Communication in only one direction.

simulate To represent the function of a device, system, or program with another device, system, or program.

single step Operation of a computer in such a manner that only one instruction is executed each time that the computer is started.

software The collection of programs and routines associated with a computer.

sort The process of placing a list in order; *see* Binary radix sort, Bubble sort, Comparative sort, Distributive sort, External sort, Internal sort, Merge sort, Quickersort, Radix sort, Selection sort, Tree sort.

sort effort The number of comparisons or moves needed to order an unordered list.

source language *See* Language, source.

source program A computer program written in a source language.

space The state of a communication channel corresponding to a binary zero. The spacing condition exists when no current flows (no hole in paper tape) on a current-loop channel, or when the voltage is more positive that +3 volts on an EIA RS–232–C channel.

spanning tree A subgraph of a graph with two properties: First, it is a tree, and second, it contains all the nodes of the original graph.

sparse array An array in which most of the entries have a value of zero.

stack A list that restricts insertions and deletions to one end.

start bit A bit used in asynchronous transmission to precede the first bit of a character transmitted serially, signaling the start of the character.

statement An expression or instruction in a source language.

stop bit A bit (or bits) used in asynchronous transmission to signal the end of a character transmitted serially, and representing the quiescent state in which the line will remain until the next character begins.

stop code A control character which, in the case of a teletype, turns off the paper tape reader.

storage allocation The assignment of blocks of data and instructions to specified blocks of storage.

storage capacity The amount of data that can be contained in a storage device.

storage device A device in which data can be entered, retained, and retrieved.
store To enter data into a storage device.
string A series of characters stored in a contiguous area in memory.
structure The organization or arrangement of the parts of an entity.
subroutine, closed A subroutine not stored in the main part of a program; such a subroutine is normally called or entered with a branch instruction, and provision is made to return control to the main routine at the end of the subroutine.
subroutine, open A subroutine that must be relocated and inserted into a routine at each place it is used.
subscript One of a set of characters used to index the location of item in an array.
swapping In a time-sharing environment, the action of either temporarily bringing a user program into main memory or storing it on a system device.
switch A device or programming technique for making selections.
symbol table A table in which symbols and their corresponding values are recorded.
symbolic address A set of characters used to specify a memory location within a program.
symbolic editor A system program which helps users in the preparation and modification of source language programs by adding, changing, or deleting lines of text.
sync character A character transmitted to establish character synchronization in synchronous communication. When the receiving station recognizes the sync character, the receiving station is said to be synchronized with the transmitting station, and communication can begin.
synchronous transmission A mode of transmission using that synchronizes a character stream with a time bit stream.
synonym Two or more keys that produce the same table address when hashed.
system A combination of software and hardware that performs specific processing operations.

table A collection of data stored for ease of reference, usually as an array.
tail A special data item that locates the end of a list.
tariff A published schedule of regulated charges for common carrier services and equipment.
teleprinter An automatic printing device operated by electrically coded signals from a keyboard.
teleprocessing system Data processing equipment used in combination with terminal equipment and communication facilities.
teletype Any of several configurations of keyboards, printers, and paper-tape equipment manufactured by the Teletype Corporation.
telpak A type of communication link provided by common carriers that represents a band of frequencies which can be subdivided into voice and data channels of various bandwidths.
temporary storage Storage locations reserved for immediate results.
terminal A peripheral device in a system through which data can enter or leave the computer.

terminal node A node of a tree which has no successors.

test for alphabetic A check that guarantees correct alphabetic input.

test for blanks In this test, an indication must be made as to which fields must be blank. If the field requires blanks, a constant of the proper number of blanks is compared against the field, and a test made for an equal condition. An unequal comparison indicates an error condition.

test for numeric A test of a numeric field to ensure against its having interspersed blanks and/or extraneous zone bits. Blanks are replaced by zeros. If the numeric field may not contain zone bits, zones are stripped from the field by the appropriate instructions.

test for sign A check made to ensure that the proper algebraic sign is present for the type of transaction involved.

text editor A program that assists in the preparation of text.

threaded tree A tree containing additional pointers to assist in the scan of the tree.

time division multiplexing The merging of several bit streams of lower bit rates into a composite signal for transmission over a communication channel of higher bit-rate capacity. Example: five bit streams operating at 100 bps might be accommodated on a channel having a capacity of 500 bps. Combining the data streams is accomplished by assigning a "time-slice" of the high-speed channel to each of the low-speed channels.

time quantum In time-sharing, a unit of time allotted to each user by the monitor.

timesharing A method of allocating central processor time and other computer resources to multiple users so that the computer, in effect, apparently processes a number of programs simultaneously.

toggle To use switches to enter data into the computer memory.

token A code or symbol representing a name or entity in a programming language.

track The portion of a magnetic storage medium which passes under a positioned read/write head.

traffic intensity The ratio of insertion rate to the deletion rate of a queue.

transducer A device that converts information in one form into information in another form.

translate To convert from one language to another.

tree A connected graph with no cycles. A *directed tree* is a directed graph that contains no cycles and no alternate paths; it has a unique node (the root) whose successor set consists of all the other nodes.

tree sort A sort that exchanges items treated as nodes of a tree. When an item reaches the root nóde, it is exchanged with the lowest leaf node. (Also called *heap sort.*).

truncation The reduction of precision by dropping one or more of the least significant digits; for example, 3.141592 truncated to four decimal digits is 3.141.

unattended operation Transmission and/or reception without an operator.

underflow An act that occurs when an attempt is made to access an item in a data structure that contains no items; contrast with Overflow.

update A method to modify a master file with current information, according to a specified procedure.

USASCII An abbreviation for United States of America Standard Code for Information Interchange, a specific code using seven bits to represent a character.

user Programmer or operator of a computer.

variable A symbol whose value changes during the execution of a program.

vector In computer science, a data structure that permits the location of any item by the use of a single index or subscript; contrast with a table, or matrix, which requires two subscripts to locate an item uniquely.

voice-grade channel Typically, a telephone circuit used for speech communication and accommodating frequencies from 300 to 3,000 Hz.

VRC Vertical Redundancy Check (*see* Parity).

white noise Noise (electrical or acoustical) whose energy spectrum is uniformly distributed across all frequencies within a band of interest.

wideband channel A communication channel having a bandwidth greater than that of a voice-grade line and usually some multiple of the bandwidth of a voice-grade line.

word A unit of data that may be stored in one addressable location.

WPM Words Per Minute; a measure of transmission speed.

wrap data The transmission of data through a communications system and the return of the data to its source to test the accuracy of the system.

write To transfer information from main memory to a peripheral device or to auxiliary storage.

INDEX